T0261646

Understanding and Using C Pointers

Richard Reese

Beijing · Cambridge · Farnham · Köln · Sebastopol · Tokyo

Understanding and Using C Pointers

by Richard Reese

Copyright © 2013 Richard Reese, Ph.D. All rights reserved.

Printed in the United States of America.

Published by O'Reilly Media, Inc., 1005 Gravenstein Highway North, Sebastopol, CA 95472.

O'Reilly books may be purchased for educational, business, or sales promotional use. Online editions are also available for most titles (*http://my.safaribooksonline.com*). For more information, contact our corporate/institutional sales department: 800-998-9938 or *corporate@oreilly.com*.

Editors: Simon St. Laurent and Nathan Jepson	**Indexer:** Potomac Indexing, LLC, Angela Howard
Production Editor: Rachel Steely	**Cover Designer:** Karen Montgomery
Copyeditor: Andre Barnett	**Interior Designer:** David Futato
Proofreader: Rachel Leach	**Illustrator:** Kara Ebrahim

May 2013:   First Edition

Revision History for the First Edition:

2013-04-30:   First release

2014-04-04:   Second release

See *http://oreilly.com/catalog/errata.csp?isbn=9781449344184* for release details.

Nutshell Handbook, the Nutshell Handbook logo, and the O'Reilly logo are registered trademarks of O'Reilly Media, Inc. *Understanding and Using C Pointers*, the image of a piping crow, and related trade dress are trademarks of O'Reilly Media, Inc.

Many of the designations used by manufacturers and sellers to distinguish their products are claimed as trademarks. Where those designations appear in this book, and O'Reilly Media, Inc., was aware of a trademark claim, the designations have been printed in caps or initial caps.

While every precaution has been taken in the preparation of this book, the publisher and author assume no responsibility for errors or omissions, or for damages resulting from the use of the information contained herein.

ISBN: 978-1-449-34418-4

[LSI]

Table of Contents

Preface

C is an important language and has had extensive treatment over the years. Central to the language are pointers that provide much of the flexibility and power found in the language. It provides the mechanism to dynamically manipulate memory, enhances support for data structures, and enables access to hardware. This power and flexibility comes with a price: pointers can be difficult to master.

Why This Book Is Different

Numerous books have been written about C. They usually offer a broad coverage of the language while addressing pointers only to the extent necessary for the topic at hand. Rarely do they venture beyond a basic treatment of pointers and most give only cursory coverage of the important memory management technology involving the stack and the heap. Yet without this discussion, only an incomplete understanding of pointers can be obtained. The stack and heap are areas of memory used to support functions and dynamic memory allocation, respectively.

Pointers are complex enough to deserve more in-depth treatment. This book provides that treatment by focusing on pointers to convey a deeper understanding of C. Part of this understanding requires a working knowledge of the program stack and heap along with the use of pointers in this context. Any area of knowledge can be understood at varying degrees, ranging from a cursory overview to an in-depth, intuitive understanding. That higher level of understanding for C can only be achieved with a solid understanding of pointers and the management of memory.

The Approach

Programming is concerned with manipulating data that is normally located in memory. It follows that a better understanding of how C manages memory will provide insight that translates to better programming. While it is one thing to know that the `malloc` function allocates memory from the heap, it is another thing to understand the implications of this allocation. If we allocate a structure whose logical size is 45, we may be surprised to learn that more than 45 bytes are typically allocated and the memory allocated may be fragmented.

When a function is called, a stack frame is created and pushed onto the program stack. Understanding stack frames and the program stack will clarify the concepts of passing by value and passing by pointer. While not necessarily directly related to pointers, the understanding of stack frames also explains how recursion works.

To facilitate the understanding of pointers and memory management techniques, various memory models will be presented. These range from a simple linear representation of memory to more complex diagrams that illustrate the state of the program stack and heap for a specific example. Code displayed on a screen or in a book is a static representation of a dynamic program. The abstract nature of this representation is a major stumbling block to understanding a program's behavior. Memory models go a long way to helping bridge this gap.

Audience

The C language is a block structured language whose procedural aspects are shared with most modern languages such as C++ and Java. They all use a program stack and heap. They all use pointers, which are often disguised as references. We assume that you have a minimal understanding of C. If you are learning C, then this book will provide you with a more comprehensive treatment of pointers and memory than is found in other books. It will expand your knowledge base regarding C and highlight unfamiliar aspects of C. If you are a more experienced C or C++ programmer, this book will help you fill in possible gaps regarding C and will enhance your understanding of how they work "under the hood," thus making you a better programmer. If you are a C# or Java developer, this book will help you better understand C and provide you with insight into how object-oriented languages deal with the stack and the heap.

Organization

The book is organized along traditional topics such as arrays, structures, and functions. However, each chapter focuses on the use of pointers and how memory is managed. For example, passing and returning pointers to and from functions are covered, and we also depict their use as part of stack frames and how they reference memory in the heap.

Chapter 1, Introduction
> This chapter covers pointer basics for those who are not necessarily proficient or are new to pointers. This includes pointer operators and the declaration of different types of pointers such as constant pointers, function pointers, and the use of NULL and its closely related variations. This can have a significant impact on how memory is allocated and used.

Chapter 2, Dynamic Memory Management in C

Dynamic memory allocation is the subject of Chapter 2. The standard memory allocation functions are covered along with techniques for dealing with the deallocation of memory. Effective memory deallocation is critical to most applications, and failure to adequately address this activity can result in memory leaks and dangling pointers. Alternative deallocation techniques, including garbage collection and exception handlers, are presented.

Chapter 3, Pointers and Functions

Functions provide the building blocks for an application's code. However, passing or returning data to and from functions can be confusing to new developers. This chapter covers techniques for passing data, along with common pitfalls that occur when returning information by pointers. This is followed by extensive treatment of function pointers. These types of pointers provide yet another level of control and flexibility that can be used to enhance a program.

Chapter 4, Pointers and Arrays

While array notation and pointer notation are not completely interchangeable, they are closely related. This chapter covers single and multidimensional arrays and how pointers are used with them. In particular, passing arrays and the various nuisances involved in dynamically allocating arrays in both a contiguous and a noncontiguous manner are explained and illustrated with different memory models.

Chapter 5, Pointers and Strings

Strings are an important component of many applications. This chapter addresses the fundamentals of strings and their manipulation with pointers. The literal pool and its impact on pointers is another often neglected feature of C. Illustrations are provided to explain and illuminate this topic.

Chapter 6, Pointers and Structures

Structures provide a very useful way of ordering and manipulating data. Pointers enhance the utility of structures by providing more flexibility in how they can be constructed. This chapter presents the basics of structures as they relate to memory allocation and pointers, followed by examples of how they can be used with various data structures.

Chapter 7, Security Issues and the Improper Use of Pointers

As powerful and useful as pointers can be, they are also the source of many security problems. In this chapter, we examine the fundamental problems surrounding buffer overflow and related pointer issues. Techniques for mitigating many of these problems are presented.

Chapter 8, Odds and Ends
> The last chapter addresses other pointer techniques and issues. While C is not an object-oriented language, many aspects of object-oriented programming can be incorporated into a C program, including polymorphic behavior. The essential elements of using pointers with threads are illustrated. The meaning and use of the `restrict` keyword are covered.

Summary

This book is intended to provide a more in-depth discussion of the use of pointers than is found in other books. It presents examples ranging from the core use of pointers to obscure uses of pointers and identifies common pointer problems.

Conventions Used in This Book

The following typographical conventions are used in this book:

Italic
> Indicates new terms, URLs, email addresses, filenames, and file extensions.

`Constant width`
> Used for program listings, as well as within paragraphs to refer to program elements such as variable or function names, databases, data types, environment variables, statements, and keywords.

`Constant width bold`
> Shows commands or other text that should be typed literally by the user.

`Constant width italic`
> Shows text that should be replaced with user-supplied values or by values determined by context.

 This icon signifies a tip, suggestion, or general note.

 This icon indicates a warning or caution.

Using Code Examples

This book is here to help you get your job done. In general, if this book includes code examples, you may use the code in your programs and documentation. You do not need to contact us for permission unless you're reproducing a significant portion of the code. For example, writing a program that uses several chunks of code from this book does not require permission. Selling or distributing a CD-ROM of examples from O'Reilly books does require permission. Answering a question by citing this book and quoting example code does not require permission. Incorporating a significant amount of example code from this book into your product's documentation does require permission.

We appreciate, but do not require, attribution. An attribution usually includes the title, author, publisher, and ISBN. For example: "*Understanding and Using C Pointers* by Richard Reese (O'Reilly). Copyright 2013 Richard Reese, Ph.D. 978-1-449-34418-4."

If you feel your use of code examples falls outside fair use or the permission given above, feel free to contact us at *permissions@oreilly.com*.

Safari® Books Online

 Safari Books Online (*www.safaribooksonline.com*) is an on-demand digital library that delivers expert content in both book and video form from the world's leading authors in technology and business.

Technology professionals, software developers, web designers, and business and creative professionals use Safari Books Online as their primary resource for research, problem solving, learning, and certification training.

Safari Books Online offers a range of product mixes and pricing programs for organizations, government agencies, and individuals. Subscribers have access to thousands of books, training videos, and prepublication manuscripts in one fully searchable database from publishers like O'Reilly Media, Prentice Hall Professional, Addison-Wesley Professional, Microsoft Press, Sams, Que, Peachpit Press, Focal Press, Cisco Press, John Wiley & Sons, Syngress, Morgan Kaufmann, IBM Redbooks, Packt, Adobe Press, FT Press, Apress, Manning, New Riders, McGraw-Hill, Jones & Bartlett, Course Technology, and dozens more. For more information about Safari Books Online, please visit us online.

How to Contact Us

Please address comments and questions concerning this book to the publisher:

O'Reilly Media, Inc.
1005 Gravenstein Highway North
Sebastopol, CA 95472
800-998-9938 (in the United States or Canada)
707-829-0515 (international or local)
707-829-0104 (fax)

We have a web page for this book, where we list errata, examples, and any additional information. You can access this page at *http://oreil.ly/Understand_Use_CPointers*.

To comment or ask technical questions about this book, send email to *bookquestions@oreilly.com*.

For more information about our books, courses, conferences, and news, see our website at *http://www.oreilly.com*.

Find us on Facebook: *http://facebook.com/oreilly*

Follow us on Twitter: *http://twitter.com/oreillymedia*

Watch us on YouTube: *http://www.youtube.com/oreillymedia*

CHAPTER 1

Introduction

A solid understanding of pointers and the ability to effectively use them separates a novice C programmer from a more experienced one. Pointers pervade the language and provide much of its flexibility. They provide important support for dynamic memory allocation, are closely tied to array notation, and, when used to point to functions, add another dimension to flow control in a program.

Pointers have long been a stumbling block in learning C. The basic concept of a pointer is simple: it is a variable that stores the address of a memory location. The concept, however, quickly becomes complicated when we start applying pointer operators and try to discern their often cryptic notations. But this does not have to be the case. If we start simple and establish a firm foundation, then the advanced uses of pointers are not hard to follow and apply.

The key to comprehending pointers is understanding how memory is managed in a C program. After all, pointers contain addresses in memory. If we don't understand how memory is organized and managed, it is difficult to understand how pointers work. To address this concern, the organization of memory is illustrated whenever it is useful to explain a pointer concept. Once you have a firm grasp of memory and the ways it can be organized, understanding pointers becomes a lot easier.

This chapter presents an introduction to pointers, their operators, and how they interact with memory. The first section examines how they are declared, the basic pointer operators, and the concept of null. There are various types of "nulls" supported by C so a careful examination of them can be enlightening.

The second section looks more closely at the various memory models you will undoubtedly encounter when working with C. The model used with a given compiler and operating system environment affects how pointers are used. In addition, we closely examine various predefined types related to pointers and the memory models.

Pointer operators are covered in more depth in the next section, including pointer arithmetic and pointer comparisons. The last section examines constants and pointers. The numerous declaration combinations offer many interesting and often very useful possibilities.

Whether you are a novice C programmer or an experienced programmer, this book will provide you with a solid understanding of pointers and fill the gaps in your education. The experienced programmer will want to pick and choose the topics of interest. The beginning programmer should probably take a more deliberate approach.

Pointers and Memory

When a C program is compiled, it works with three types of memory:

Static/Global

Statically declared variables are allocated to this type of memory. Global variables also use this region of memory. They are allocated when the program starts and remain in existence until the program terminates. While all functions have access to global variables, the scope of static variables is restricted to their defining function.

Automatic

These variables are declared within a function and are created when a function is called. Their scope is restricted to the function, and their lifetime is limited to the time the function is executing.

Dynamic

Memory is allocated from the heap and can be released as necessary. A pointer references the allocated memory. The scope is limited to the pointer or pointers that reference the memory. It exists until it is released. This is the focus of Chapter 2.

Table 1-1 summarizes the scope of and lifetime of variables used in these memory regions.

Table 1-1. Scope and lifetime

	Scope	Lifetime
Global	The entire file	The lifetime of the application
Static	The function it is declared within	The lifetime of the application
Automatic (local)	The function it is declared within	While the function is executing
Dynamic	Determined by the pointers that reference this memory	Until the memory is freed

Understanding these types of memory will enable you to better understand how pointers work. Most pointers are used to manipulate data in memory. Understanding how memory is partitioned and organized will clarify how pointers manipulate memory.

A pointer variable contains the address in memory of another variable, object, or function. An object is considered to be memory allocated using one of the memory allocation functions, such as the `malloc` function. A pointer is normally declared to be of a specific type depending on what it points to, such as a pointer to a `char`. The object may be any C data type such as integer, character, string, or structure. However, nothing inherent in a pointer indicates what type of data the pointer is referencing. A pointer only contains an address.

Why You Should Become Proficient with Pointers

Pointers have several uses, including:

- Creating fast and efficient code
- Providing a convenient means for addressing many types of problems
- Supporting dynamic memory allocation
- Making expressions compact and succinct
- Providing the ability to pass data structures by pointer without incurring a large overhead
- Protecting data passed as a parameter to a function

Faster and more efficient code can be written because pointers are closer to the hardware. That is, the compiler can more easily translate the operation into machine code. There is not as much overhead associated with pointers as might be present with other operators.

Many data structures are more easily implemented using pointers. For example, a linked list could be supported using either arrays or pointers. However, pointers are easier to use and map directly to a next or previous link. An array implementation requires array indexes that are not as intuitive or as flexible as pointers.

Figure 1-1 illustrates how this can be visualized using arrays and pointers for a linked list of employees. The lefthand side of the figure uses an array. The head variable indicates that the linked list's first element is at index 10 of the array. Each array's element contains a structure that represents an employee. The structure's `next` field holds the index in the array of the next employee. The shaded elements represent unused array elements.

The righthand side shows the equivalent representation using pointers. The head variable holds a pointer to the first employee's node. Each node holds employee data as well as a pointer to the next node in the linked list.

The pointer representation is not only clearer but also more flexible. The size of an array typically needs to be known when it is created. This will impose a restriction on the number of elements it can hold. The pointer representation does not suffer from this limitation as a new node can be dynamically allocated as needed.

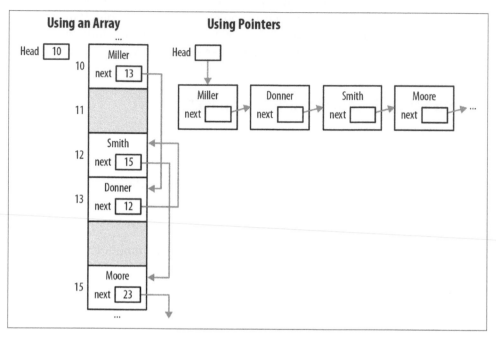

Figure 1-1. Array versus pointers representation of a linked list

Dynamic memory allocation is effected in C through the use of pointers. The malloc and free functions are used to allocate and release dynamic memory, respectively. Dynamic memory allocation enables variable-sized arrays and data structures, such as linked lists and queues. However, in the new C standard, C11, variable size arrays are supported.

Compact expressions can be very descriptive but can also be cryptic, as pointer notation is not always fully understood by many programmers. Compact expressions should address a specific need and not be cryptic just to be cryptic. For example, in the following sequence, the third character of the names' second element is displayed with two different printf functions. If this usage of pointers is confusing, don't worry—we will explain how dereferencing works in more detail in the section "Dereferencing a Pointer Using the Indirection Operator" on page 11. While the two approaches are equivalent and will display the character n, the simpler approach is to use array notation.

```
char *names[] = {"Miller","Jones","Anderson"};
printf("%c\n",*(*(names+1)+2));
printf("%c\n",names[1][2]);
```

Pointers represent a powerful tool to create and enhance applications. On the downside, many problems can occur when using pointers, such as:

- Accessing arrays and other data structures beyond their bounds
- Referencing automatic variables after they have gone out of existence
- Referencing heap allocated memory after it has been released
- Dereferencing a pointer before memory has been allocated to it

These types of problems will be examined in more detail in Chapter 7.

The syntax and semantics of pointer usage are fairly well defined in the C specification (*http://bit.ly/173cDxJ*). However, there are situations where the specification does not explicitly define pointer behavior. In these cases the behavior is defined to be either:

Implementation-defined
Some specific, documented implementation is provided. An example of implementation-defined behavior is how the high-order bit is propagated in an integer shift right operation.

Unspecified
Some implementation is provided but is not documented. An example of an unspecified behavior is the amount of memory allocated by the `malloc` function with an argument of zero. A list of unspecified behavior can be found at CERT Secure Coding Appendix DD (*http://bit.ly/YOFY8s*).

Undefined
There are no requirements imposed and anything can happen. An example of this is the value of a pointer deallocated by the `free` functions. A list of undefined behavior can be found at CERT Secure Coding Appendix CC (*http://bit.ly/16msOVK*).

Sometimes there are locale-specific behaviors. These are usually documented by the compiler vendor. Providing locale-specific behavior allows the compiler-writer latitude in generating more efficient code.

Declaring Pointers

Pointer variables are declared using a data type followed by an asterisk and then the pointer variable's name. In the following example, an integer and a pointer to an integer are declared:

```
int num;
int *pi;
```

The use of white spaces around the asterisk is irrelevant. The following declarations are all equivalent:

```
int* pi;
int * pi;
int *pi;
int*pi;
```

 The use of white space is a matter of user preference.

The asterisk declares the variable as a pointer. It is an overloaded symbol as it is also used for multiplication and dereferencing a pointer.

Figure 1-2 illustrates how memory would typically be allocated for the above declaration. Three memory locations are depicted by the three rectangles. The number to the left of each rectangle is its address. The name next to the address is the variable assigned to this location. The address 100 is used here for illustrative purposes. The actual address of a pointer, or any variable for that matter, is not normally known, nor is its value of interest in most applications. The three dots represent uninitialized memory.

Pointers to uninitialized memory can be a problem. If such a pointer is dereferenced, the pointer's content probably does not represent a valid address, and if it does, it may not contain valid data. An invalid address is one that the program is not authorized to access. This will result in the program terminating on most platforms, which is significant and can lead to a number of problems, as discussed in Chapter 7.

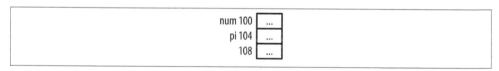

Figure 1-2. Memory diagram

The variables num and pi are located at addresses 100 and 104, respectively. Both are assumed to occupy four bytes. Both of these sizes will differ, depending on the system configuration as addressed in the section "Pointer Size and Types" on page 15. Unless otherwise noted, we will use four-byte integers for all of our examples.

 In this book, we will use an address such as 100 to explain how pointers work. This will simplify the examples. When you execute the examples you will get different addresses, and these addresses can even change between repeated executions of the program.

There are several points to remember:

- The content of `pi` should eventually be assigned the address of an integer variable.
- These variables have not been initialized and thus contain garbage.
- There is nothing inherent to a pointer's implementation that suggests what type of data it is referencing or whether its contents are valid.
- However, the pointer type has been specified and the compiler will frequently complain when the pointer is not used correctly.

 By garbage, we mean the memory allocation could contain any value. When memory is allocated it is not cleared. The previous contents could be anything. If the previous contents held a floating point number, interpreting it as an integer would likely not be useful. Even if it contained an integer, it would not likely be the right integer. Thus, its contents are said to hold garbage.

While a pointer may be used without being initialized, it may not always work properly until it has been initialized.

How to Read a Declaration

Now is a good time to suggest a way to read pointer declarations, which can make them easier to understand. The trick is to read them backward. While we haven't discussed pointers to constants yet, let's examine the following declaration:

```
const int *pci;
```

Reading the declaration backward allows us to progressively understand the declaration (Figure 1-3).

1. `pci` is a variable	const int ***pci;**
2. `pci` is a pointer variable	const int ***pci;**
3. `pci` is a pointer variable to an integer	const **int *pci;**
4. `pci` is a pointer variable to a constant integer	**const int *pci;**

Figure 1-3. The backward declaration

Many programmers find that reading the declaration backward is less complex.

When working with complex pointer expressions, draw a picture of them, as we will do in many of our examples.

Address of Operator

The address of operator, &, will return its operand's address. We can initialize the pi pointer with the address of num using this operator as follows:

```
num = 0;
pi = &num;
```

The variable num is set to zero, and pi is set to point to the address of num as illustrated in Figure 1-4.

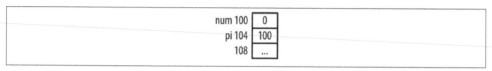

num 100 | 0
pi 104 | 100
108 | ...

Figure 1-4. Memory assignments

We could have initialized pi to point to the address of num when the variables were declared as illustrated below:

```
int num;
int *pi = &num;
```

Using these declarations, the following statement will result in a syntax error on most compilers:

```
num = 0;
pi = num;
```

The error would appear as follows:

```
error: invalid conversion from 'int' to 'int*'
```

The variable pi is of type pointer to an integer and num is of type integer. The error message is saying we cannot convert an integer to a pointer to the data type integer.

 Assignment of integers to a pointer will generally cause a warning or error.

Pointers and integers are not the same. They may both be stored using the same number of bytes on most machines, but they are not the same. However, it is possible to cast an integer to a pointer to an integer:

```
pi = (int *)num;
```

This will not generate a syntax error. When executed, though, the program may terminate abnormally when the program attempts to dereference the value at address zero. An address of zero is not always valid for use in a program on most operating systems. We will discuss this in more detail in the section "The Concept of Null" on page 11.

It is a good practice to initialize a pointer as soon as possible, as illustrated below:

```
int num;
int *pi;
pi = &num;
```

Displaying Pointer Values

Rarely will the variables we use actually have an address such as 100 and 104. However, the variable's address can be determined by printing it out as follows:

```
int num = 0;
int *pi = &num;

printf("Address of num: %d  Value: %d\n",&num, num);
printf("Address of pi: %d  Value: %d\n",&pi, pi);
```

When executed, you may get output as follows. We used real addresses in this example. Your addresses will probably be different:

```
Address of num: 4520836  Value: 0
Address of pi: 4520824  Value: 4520836
```

The printf function has a couple of other field specifiers useful when displaying pointer values, as summarized in Table 1-2.

Table 1-2. Field specifiers

Specifier	Meaning
%x	Displays the value as a hexadecimal number.
%o	Displays the value as an octal number.
%p	Displays the value in an implementation-specific manner; typically as a hexadecimal number.

Their use is demonstrated below:

```
printf("Address of pi: %d  Value: %d\n",&pi, pi);
printf("Address of pi: %x  Value: %x\n",&pi, pi);
```

```
printf("Address of pi: %o  Value: %o\n",&pi, pi);
printf("Address of pi: %p  Value: %p\n",&pi, pi);
```

This will display the address and contents of pi, as shown below. In this case, pi holds the address of num:

```
Address of pi: 4520824  Value: 4520836
Address of pi: 44fb78  Value: 44fb84
Address of pi: 21175570  Value: 21175604
Address of pi: 0044FB78  Value: 0044FB84
```

The %p specifier differs from %x as it typically displays the hexadecimal number in uppercase. We will use the %p specifier for addresses unless otherwise indicated.

Displaying pointer values consistently on different platforms can be challenging. One approach is to cast the pointer as a pointer to void and then display it using the %p format specifier as follows:

```
printf("Value of pi: %p\n", (void*)pi);
```

Pointers to void is explained in "Pointer to void" on page 14. To keep our examples simple, we will use the %p specifier and not cast the address to a pointer to void.

Virtual memory and pointers

To further complicate displaying addresses, the pointer addresses displayed on a *virtual operating system* are not likely to be the real physical memory addresses. A virtual operating system allows a program to be split across the machine's physical address space. An application is split into pages/frames. These pages represent areas of main memory. The pages of the application are allocated to different, potentially noncontiguous areas of memory and may not all be in memory at the same time. If the operating system needs memory currently held by a page, the memory may be swapped out to secondary storage and then reloaded at a later time, frequently at a different memory location. These capabilities provide a virtual operating system with considerable flexibility in how it manages memory.

Each program assumes it has access to the machine's entire physical memory space. In reality, it does not. The address used by a program is a virtual address. The operating system maps the virtual address to a real physical memory address when needed.

This means code and data in a page may be in different physical locations as the program executes. The application's virtual addresses do not change; they are the addresses we see when we examine the contents of a pointer. The virtual addresses are transparently mapped to real addresses by the operating system.

The operating system handles all of this, and it is not something that the programmer has control over or needs to worry about. Understanding these issues explains the addresses returned by a program running in a virtual operating system.

Dereferencing a Pointer Using the Indirection Operator

The indirection operator, *, returns the value pointed to by a pointer variable. This is frequently referred to as dereferencing a pointer. In the following example, num and pi are declared and initialized:

```
int num = 5;
int *pi = &num;
```

The indirection operator is then used in the following statement to display 5, the value of num:

```
printf("%p\n",*pi);    // Displays 5
```

We can also use the result of the dereference operator as an *lvalue*. The term lvalue refers to the operand found on the left side of the assignment operator. All `lvalues` must be modifiable since they are being assigned a value.

The following will assign 200 to the integer pointed to by pi. Since it is pointing to the variable num, 200 will be assigned to num. Figure 1-5 illustrates how memory is affected:

```
*pi = 200;
printf("%d\n",num);    // Displays 200
```

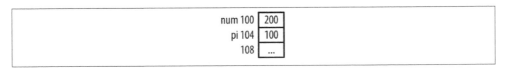

Figure 1-5. Memory assigned using dereference operator

Pointers to Functions

A pointer can be declared to point to a function. The declaration notation is a bit cryptic. The following illustrates how to declare a pointer to a function. The function is passed void and returns void. The pointer's name is foo:

```
void (*foo)();
```

A *pointer* to a function is a rich topic area and will be covered in more detail in Chapter 3.

The Concept of Null

The concept of null is interesting and sometimes misunderstood. Confusion can occur because we often deal with several similar, yet distinct concepts, including:

- The null concept
- The null pointer constant
- The NULL macro

- The ASCII NUL
- A null string
- The null statement

When NULL is assigned to a pointer, it means the pointer does not point to anything. The null concept refers to the idea that a pointer can hold a special value that is not equal to another pointer. It does not point to any area of memory. Two null pointers will always be equal to each other. There can be a null pointer type for each pointer type, such as a pointer to a character or a pointer to an integer, although this is uncommon.

The null concept is an abstraction supported by the null pointer constant. This constant may or may not be a constant zero. A C programmer need not be concerned with their actual internal representation.

The NULL macro is a constant integer zero cast to a pointer to void. In many libraries, it is defined as follows:

```
#define NULL    ((void *)0)
```

This is what we typically think of as a null pointer. Its definition frequently can be found within several different header files, including *stddef.h*, *stdlib.h*, and *stdio.h*.

If a nonzero bit pattern is used by the compiler to represent null, then it is the compiler's responsibility to ensure all uses of NULL or 0 in a pointer context are treated as null pointers. The actual internal representation of null is implementation-defined. The use of NULL and 0 are language-level symbols that represent a null pointer.

The ASCII NUL is defined as a byte containing all zeros. However, this is not the same as a null pointer. A string in C is represented as a sequence of characters terminated by a zero value. The null string is an empty string and does not contain any characters. Finally, the null statement consists of a statement with a single semicolon.

As we will see, a null pointer is a very useful feature for many data structure implementations, such as a linked list where it is often used to mark the end of the list.

If the intent was to assign the null value to pi, we use the NULL type as follows:

```
pi = NULL;
```

 A null pointer and an uninitialized pointer are different. An uninitialized pointer can contain any value, whereas a pointer containing NULL does not reference any location in memory.

Interestingly, we can assign a zero to a pointer, but we cannot assign any other integer value. Consider the following assignment operations:

```
        pi = 0;
        pi = NULL;
        pi = 100;      // Syntax error
        pi = num;      // Syntax error
```

A pointer can be used as the sole operand of a logical expression. For example, we can test to see whether the pointer is set to NULL using the following sequence:

```
        if(pi) {
            // Not NULL
        } else {
            // Is NULL
        }
```

 Either of the two following expressions are valid but are redundant. It may be clearer, but explicit comparison to NULL is not necessary.

If pi has been assigned a NULL value in this context, then it will be interpreted as the binary zero. Since this represents false in C, the else clause will be executed if pi contains NULL.

```
        if(pi == NULL) ...
        if(pi != NULL) ...
```

 A null pointer should never be dereferenced because it does not contain a valid address. When executed it will result in the program terminating.

To NULL or not to NULL

Which is better form: using NULL or using 0 when working with pointers? Either is perfectly acceptable; the choice is one of preference. Some developers prefer to use NULL because it is a reminder that we are working with pointers. Others feel this is unnecessary because the zero is simply hidden.

However, NULL should not be used in contexts other than pointers. It might work some of the time, but it is not intended to be used this way. It can definitely be a problem when used in place of the ASCII NUL character. This character is not defined in any standard C header file. It is equivalent to the character literal, '\0', which evaluates to the decimal value zero.

The meaning of zero changes depending on its context. It might mean the integer zero in some contexts, and it might mean a null pointer in a different context. Consider the following example:

```
int num;
int *pi = 0;     // Zero refers to the null pointer,NULL
pi = &num;
*pi = 0;         // Zero refers to the integer zero
```

We are accustomed to overloaded operators, such as the asterisk used to declare a pointer, to dereference a pointer, or to multiply. The zero is also overloaded. We may find this discomforting because we are not used to overloading operands.

Pointer to void

A pointer to void is a general-purpose pointer used to hold references to any data type. An example of a pointer to void is shown below:

```
void *pv;
```

It has two interesting properties:

- A pointer to void will have the same representation and memory alignment as a pointer to char.

- A pointer to void will never be equal to another pointer. However, two void pointers assigned a NULL value will be equal. The actual behavior of void pointers is system dependent.

Any pointer can be assigned to a pointer to void. It can then be cast back to its original pointer type. When this happens the value will be equal to the original pointer value. This is illustrated in the following sequence, where a pointer to int is assigned to a pointer to void and then back to a pointer to int:

```
int num;
int *pi = &num;
printf("Value of pi: %p\n", pi);
void* pv = pi;
pi = (int*) pv;
printf("Value of pi: %p\n", pi);
```

When this sequence is executed as shown below, the pointer address is the same:

```
Value of pi: 100
Value of pi: 100
```

Pointers to void are used for data pointers, not function pointers. In "Polymorphism in C" on page 194, we will reexamine the use of pointers to void to address polymorphic behavior.

 Be careful when using pointers to void. If you cast an arbitrary pointer to a pointer to void, there is nothing preventing you from casting it to a different pointer type.

The `sizeof` operator can be used with a pointer to void. However, we cannot use the operator with void as shown below:

```
size_t size = sizeof(void*);    // Legal
size_t size = sizeof(void);     // Illegal
```

The `size_t` is a data type used for sizes and is discussed in the section "Predefined Pointer-Related Types" on page 16.

Global and static pointers

If a pointer is declared as global or static, it is initialized to NULL when the program starts. An example of a global and static pointer follows:

```
int *globalpi;

void foo() {
    static int *staticpi;
    ...
}

int main() {
    ...
}
```

Figure 1-6 illustrates this memory layout. Stack frames are pushed onto the stack, and the heap is used for dynamic memory allocation. The region above the heap is used for static/global variables. This is a conceptual diagram only. Static and global variables are frequently placed in a data segment separate from the data segment used by the stack and heap. The stack and heap are discussed in "Program Stack and Heap" on page 58.

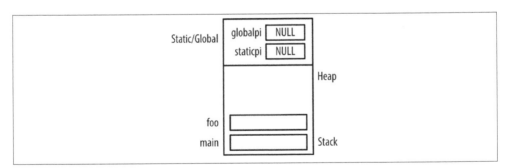

Figure 1-6. Memory allocation for global and static pointers

Pointer Size and Types

Pointer size is an issue when we become concerned about application compatibility and portability. On most modern platforms, the size of a pointer to data is normally the same regardless of the pointer type. A pointer to a char has the same size as a pointer to a structure. While the C standard does not dictate that size be the same for all data types, this is usually the case. However, the size of a pointer to a function may be different from the size of a pointer to data.

The size of a pointer depends on the machine in use and the compiler. For example, on modern versions of Windows the pointer is 32 or 64 bits in length. For DOS and Windows 3.1 operating systems, pointers were 16 or 32 bits in length.

Memory Models

The introduction of 64-bit machines has made more apparent the differences in the size of memory allocated for data types. With different machines and compilers come different options for allocating space to C primitive data types. A common notation used to describe different data models is summarized below:

    I In L Ln LL LLn P Pn

Each capital letter corresponds to an integer, long, or pointer. The lowercase letters represent the number of bits allocated for the data type. Table 1-3[1] summarizes these models, where the number is the size in bits:

Table 1-3. Machine memory models

C Data Type	LP64	ILP64	LLP64	ILP32	LP32
char	8	8	8	8	8
short	16	16	16	16	16
_int32		32			
int	32	64	32	32	16
long	64	64	32	32	32
long long			64		
pointer	64	64	64	32	32

The model depends on the operating system and compiler. More than one model may be supported on the same operating system; this is often controlled through compiler options.

Predefined Pointer-Related Types

Four predefined types are frequently used when working with pointers. They include:

1. Adapted from *http://en.wikipedia.org/wiki/64-bit*.

`size_t`
   Created to provide a safe type for sizes

`ptrdiff_t`
   Created to handle pointer arithmetic

`intptr_t` *and* `uintptr_t`
   Used for storing pointer addresses

In the following sections, we will illustrate the use of each type with the exception of `ptrdiff_t`, which will be discussed in the section "Subtracting two pointers" on page 24.

Understanding size_t

The type `size_t` represents the maximum size any object can be in C. It is an unsigned integer since negative numbers do not make sense in this context. Its purpose is to provide a portable means of declaring a size consistent with the addressable area of memory available on a system. The `size_t` type is used as the return type for the `sizeof` operator and as the argument to many functions, including `malloc` and `strlen`, among others.

It is good practice to use `size_t` when declaring variables for sizes such as the number of characters and array indexes. It should be used for loop counters, indexing into arrays, and sometimes for pointer arithmetic.

The declaration of `size_t` is implementation-specific. It is found in one or more standard headers, such as *stdio.h* and *stdlib.h*, and it is typically defined as follows:

```
#ifndef __SIZE_T
#define __SIZE_T
typedef unsigned int size_t;
#endif
```

The define directives ensure it is only defined once. The actual size will depend on the implementation. Typically, on a 32-bit system, it will be 32 bits in length, while on a 64-bit system it will be 64 bits in length. Normally, the maximum possible value for `size_t` is SIZE_MAX.

Usually `size_t` can be used to store a pointer, but it is not a good idea to assume `size_t` is the same size as a pointer. As we will see in "Using the sizeof operator with pointers" on page 18, `intptr_t` is a better choice.

Be careful when printing values defined as `size_t`. These are unsigned values, and if you choose the wrong format specifier, you'll get unreliable results. The recommended format specifier is %zu. However, this is not always available. As an alternative, consider using %u or %lu.

Consider the following example, where we define a variable as a size_t and then display it using two different format specifiers:

```
size_t sizet = -5;
printf("%d\n",sizet);
printf("%zu\n",sizet);
```

Since a variable of type size_t is intended for use with positive integers, using a negative value can present problems. When we assign it a negative number and use the %d and then the %zu format specifiers, we get the following output:

```
-5
4294967291
```

The %d field interprets size_t as a signed integer. It displays a –5 because it holds a –5. The %zu field formats size_t as an unsigned integer. When –5 is interpreted as a signed integer, its high-order bit is set to one, indicating that the integer is negative. When interpreted as an unsigned number, the high-order bit is interpreted as a large power of 2. This is why we saw the large integer when we used the %zu field specifier.

A positive number will be displayed properly as shown below:

```
sizet = 5;
printf("%d\n",sizet);     // Displays 5
printf("%zu\n",sizet);    // Displays 5
```

Since size_t is unsigned, always assign a positive number to a variable of that type.

Using the sizeof operator with pointers

The sizeof operator can be used to determine the size of a pointer. The following displays the size of a pointer to char:

```
printf("Size of *char: %d\n",sizeof(char*));
```

The output follows:

```
Size of *char: 4
```

 Always use the sizeof operator when the size of a pointer is needed.

The size of a function pointer can vary. Usually, it is consistent for a given operating system and compiler combination. Many compilers support the creation of a 32-bit or 64-bit application. It is possible that the same program, compiled with different options, will use different pointer sizes.

On a Harvard architecture, the code and data are stored in different physical memory. For example, the Intel MCS-51 (8051) microcontroller is a Harvard machine. Though Intel no longer manufactures the chip, there are many binary compatible derivatives available and in use today. The Small Device C Complier (SDCC) (*http://sdcc.source forge.net/doc/sdccman.pdf*) supports this type of processor. Pointers on this machine can range from 1 to 4 bytes in length. Thus, the size of a pointer should be determined when needed, as its size is not consistent in this type of environment.

Using intptr_t and uintptr_t

The types `intptr_t` and `uintptr_t` are used for storing pointer addresses. They provide a portable and safe way of declaring pointers, and will be the same size as the underlying pointer used on the system. They are useful for converting pointers to their integer representation.

The type `uintptr_t` is the unsigned version of `intptr_t`. For most operations `intptr_t` is preferred. The type `uintptr_t` is not as flexible as `intptr_t`. The following illustrates how to use `intptr_t`:

```
int num;
intptr_t *pi = &num;
```

If we try to assign the address of an integer to a pointer of type `uintptr_t` as follows, we will get a syntax error:

```
uintptr_t *pu = &num;
```

The error follows:

```
error: invalid conversion from 'int*' to
        'uintptr_t* {aka unsigned int*}' [-fpermissive]
```

However, performing the assignment using a cast will work:

```
intptr_t *pi = &num;
uintptr_t *pu = (uintptr_t*)&num;
```

We cannot use `uintptr_t` with other data types without casting:

```
char c;
uintptr_t *pc = (uintptr_t*)&c;
```

These types should be used when portability and safety are an issue. However, we will not use them in our examples to simplify their explanations.

 Avoid casting a pointer to an integer. In the case of 64-bit pointers, information will be lost if the integer was only four bytes.

Early Intel processors used a 16-bit segmented architecture where near and far pointers were relevant. In today's virtual memory architecture, they are no longer a factor. The far and near pointers were extensions to the C standard to support segmented architecture on early Intel processors. Near pointers were only able to address about 64KB of memory at a time. Far pointers could address up to 1MB of memory but were slower than near pointers. Huge pointers were far pointers normalized so they used the highest possible segment for the address.

Pointer Operators

There are several operators available for use with pointers. So far we have examined the dereference and address-of operators. In this section, we will look closely into pointer arithmetic and comparisons. Table 1-4 summarizes the pointer operators.

Table 1-4. Pointer operators

Operator	Name	Meaning
*		Used to declare a pointer
*	Dereference	Used to dereference a pointer
->	Point-to	Used to access fields of a structure referenced by a pointer
+	Addition	Used to increment a pointer
-	Subtraction	Used to decrement a pointer
== !=	Equality, inequality	Compares two pointers
> >= < <=	Greater than, greater than or equal, less than, less than or equal	Compares two pointers
(data type)	Cast	To change the type of pointer

Pointer Arithmetic

Several arithmetic operations are performed on pointers to data. These include:

- Adding an integer to a pointer
- Subtracting an integer from a pointer
- Subtracting two pointers from each other
- Comparing pointers

These operations are not always permitted on pointers to functions.

Adding an integer to a pointer

This operation is very common and useful. When we add an integer to a pointer, the amount added is the product of the integer times the number of bytes of the underlying data type.

The size of primitive data types can vary from system to system, as discussed in "Memory Models" on page 16. However, Table 1-5 shows the common sizes found in most systems. Unless otherwise noted, these values will be used for the examples in this book.

Table 1-5. Data type sizes

Data Type	Size in Bytes
byte	1
char	1
short	2
int	4
long	8
float	4
double	8

To illustrate the effects of adding an integer to a pointer, we will use an array of integers, as shown below. Each time one is added to pi, four is added to the address. The memory allocated for these variables is illustrated in Figure 1-7. Pointers are declared with data types so that these sorts of arithmetic operations are possible. Knowledge of the data type size allows the automatic adjustment of the pointer values in a portable fashion:

```
int vector[] = {28, 41, 7};
int *pi = vector;      // pi: 100

printf("%d\n",*pi);    // Displays 28
pi += 1;               // pi: 104
printf("%d\n",*pi);    // Displays 41
pi += 1;               // pi: 108
printf("%d\n",*pi);    // Displays 7
```

 When an array name is used by itself, it returns the address of an array, which is also the address of the first element of the array:

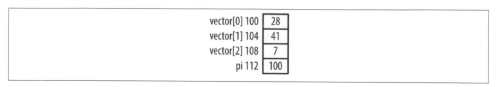

Figure 1-7. Memory allocation for vector

In the following sequence, we add three to the pointer. The variable `pi` will contain the address 112, the address of `pi`:

```
pi = vector;
pi += 3;
```

The pointer is pointing to itself. This is not very useful but illustrates the need to be careful when performing pointer arithmetic. Accessing memory past the end of an array is a dangerous thing to do and should be avoided. There is no guarantee that the memory access will be a valid variable. It is very easy to compute an invalid or useless address.

The following declarations will be used to illustrate the addition operation performed with a `short` and then a `char` data type:

```
short s;
short *ps = &s;
char c;
char *pc = &c;
```

Let's assume memory is allocated as shown in Figure 1-8. The addresses used here are all on a four-byte word boundary. Real addresses may be aligned on different boundaries and in a different order.

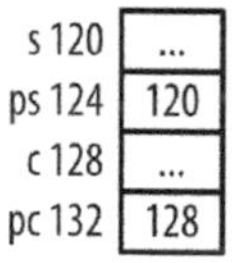

s 120	...	
ps 124	120	
c 128	...	
pc 132	128	

Figure 1-8. Pointers to short and char

The following sequence adds one to each pointer and then displays their contents:

```
printf("Content of ps before: %d\n",ps);
ps = ps + 1;
printf("Content of ps after:  %d\n",ps);

printf("Content of pc before: %d\n",pc);
pc = pc + 1;
printf("Content of pc after:  %d\n",pc);
```

When executed, you should get output similar to the following:

```
Content of ps before: 120
Content of ps after:  122
Content of pc before: 128
Address of pc after:  129
```

The ps pointer is incremented by two because the size of a short is two bytes. The pc pointer is incremented by one because its size is one byte. Again, these addresses may not contain useful information.

Pointers to void and addition

Most compilers allow arithmetic to be performed on a pointer to void as an extension. Here we will assume the size of a pointer to void is four. However, trying to add one to a pointer to void may result in a syntax error. In the following code snippet, we declare and attempt to add one to the pointer:

```
int num = 5;
void *pv = &num;
printf("%p\n",pv);
pv = pv+1;          //Syntax warning
```

The resulting warning follows:

```
warning: pointer of type 'void *' used in arithmetic [-Wpointer-arith]
```

Since this is not standard C, the compiler issued a warning. However, the resulting address contained in pv will be incremented by one byte. Most compilers will treat the data type void as if it has a size of one byte. Since the pointer points to void, the address is incremented by one.

Subtracting an integer from a pointer

Integer values can be subtracted from a pointer in the same way they are added. The size of the data type times the integer increment value is subtracted from the address. To illustrate the effects of subtracting an integer from a pointer, we will use an array of integers as shown below. The memory created for these variables is illustrated in Figure 1-7.

```
int vector[] = {28, 41, 7};
int *pi = vector + 2;  // pi: 108

printf("%d\n",*pi);    // Displays 7
pi--;                  // pi: 104
printf("%d\n",*pi);    // Displays 41
pi--;                  // pi: 100
printf("%d\n",*pi);    // Displays 28
```

Each time one is subtracted from pi, four is subtracted from the address.

Subtracting two pointers

When one pointer is subtracted from another, we get the difference between their addresses. This difference is not normally very useful except for determining the order of elements in an array.

The difference between the pointers is the number of "units" by which they differ. The difference's sign depends on the order of the operands. This is consistent with pointer addition where the number added is the pointer's data type size. We use "unit" as the operand. In the following example, we declare an array and pointers to the array's elements. We then take their difference:

```
int vector[] = {28, 41, 7};
int *p0 = vector;
int *p1 = vector+1;
int *p2 = vector+2;

printf("p2-p0:  %d\n",p2-p0);    // p2-p0:  2
printf("p2-p1:  %d\n",p2-p1);    // p2-p1:  1
printf("p0-p1:  %d\n",p0-p1);    // p0-p1:  -1
```

In the first `printf` statement, we find the difference between the positions of the array's last element and its first element is 2. That is, their indexes differ by 2. In the last `printf` statement, the difference is a –1, indicating that p0 immediately precedes the element pointed to by p1. Figure 1-9 illustrates how memory is allocated for this example.

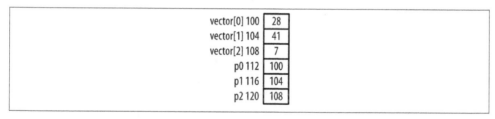

Figure 1-9. Subtracting two pointers

The type `ptrdiff_t` is a portable way to express the difference between two pointers. In the previous example, the result of subtracting two pointers is returned as a `ptrdiff_t` type. Since pointer sizes can differ, this type simplifies the task of working with their differences.

Don't confuse this technique with using the dereference operator to subtract two numbers. In the following example, we use pointers to determine the difference between the value stored in the array's first and second elements:

```
printf("*p0-*p1:  %d\n",*p0-*p1);  //  *p0-*p1:  -13
```

Comparing Pointers

Pointers can be compared using the standard comparison operators. Normally, comparing pointers is not very useful. However, when comparing pointers to elements of an array, the comparison's results can be used to determine the relative ordering of the array's elements.

We will use the vector example developed in the section "Subtracting two pointers" on page 24 to illustrate the comparison of pointers. Several comparison operators are applied to the pointers, and their results are displayed as 1 for true and 0 for false:

```
int vector[] = {28, 41, 7};
int *p0 = vector;
int *p1 = vector+1;
int *p2 = vector+2;

printf("p2>p0:  %d\n",p2>p0);    // p2>p0:  1
printf("p2<p0:  %d\n",p2<p0);    // p2<p0:  0
printf("p0>p1:  %d\n",p0>p1);    // p0>p1:  0
```

Common Uses of Pointers

Pointers can be used in a variety of ways. In this section, we will examine different ways of using pointers, including:

- Multiple levels of indirection
- Constant pointers

Multiple Levels of Indirection

Pointers can use different levels of indirection. It is not uncommon to see a variable declared as a pointer to a pointer, sometimes called a *double pointer*. A good example of this is when program arguments are passed to the main function using the traditionally named argc and argv parameters. This is discussed in more detail in Chapter 5.

The example below uses three arrays. The first array is an array of strings used to hold a list of book titles:

```
char *titles[] = {"A Tale of Two Cities",
      "Wuthering Heights","Don Quixote",
      "Odyssey","Moby-Dick","Hamlet",
      "Gulliver's Travels"};
```

Two additional arrays are provided whose purpose is to maintain a list of the "best books" and English books. Instead of holding copies of the titles, they will hold the address of a title in the titles array. Both arrays will need to be declared as a pointer to a pointer to a char. The array's elements will hold the addresses of the titles array's elements. This will avoid having to duplicate memory for each title and results in a single location for titles. If a title needs to be changed, then the change will only have to be performed in one location.

The two arrays are declared below. Each array element contains a pointer that points to a second pointer to char:

```
char **bestBooks[3];
char **englishBooks[4];
```

The two arrays are initialized and one of their elements is displayed, as shown below. In the assignment statements, the value of the righthand side is calculated by applying the subscripts first, followed by the address-of operator. For example, the second statement assigns the address of the fourth element of titles to the second element of bestBooks:

```
bestBooks[0] = &titles[0];
bestBooks[1] = &titles[3];
bestBooks[2] = &titles[5];

englishBooks[0] = &titles[0];
englishBooks[1] = &titles[1];
englishBooks[2] = &titles[5];
englishBooks[3] = &titles[6];

printf("%s\n",*englishBooks[1]);    // Wuthering Heights
```

Memory is allocated for this example as shown in Figure 1-10.

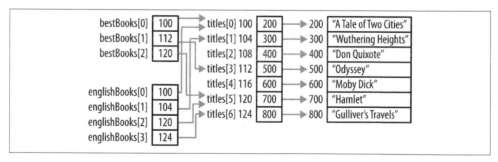

Figure 1-10. Pointers to pointers

Using multiple levels of indirection provides additional flexibility in how code can be written and used. Certain types of operations would otherwise be more difficult. In this example, if the address of a title changes, it will only require modification to the title array. We would not have to modify the other arrays.

There is not an inherent limit on the number of levels of indirection possible. Of course, using too many levels of indirection can be confusing and hard to maintain.

Constants and Pointers

Using the `const` keyword with pointers is a rich and powerful aspect of C. It provides different types of protections for different problem sets. Of particular power and usefulness is a pointer to a constant. In Chapters 3 and 5, we will see how this can protect users of a function from modification of a parameter by the function.

Pointers to a constant

A pointer can be defined to point to a constant. This means the pointer cannot be used to modify the value it is referencing. In the following example, an integer and an integer constant are declared. Next, a pointer to an integer and a pointer to an integer constant are declared and then initialized to the respective integers:

```
int num = 5;
const int limit = 500;
int *pi;                // Pointer to an integer
const int *pci;         // Pointer to a constant integer

pi = &num;
pci = &limit;
```

This is illustrated in Figure 1-11.

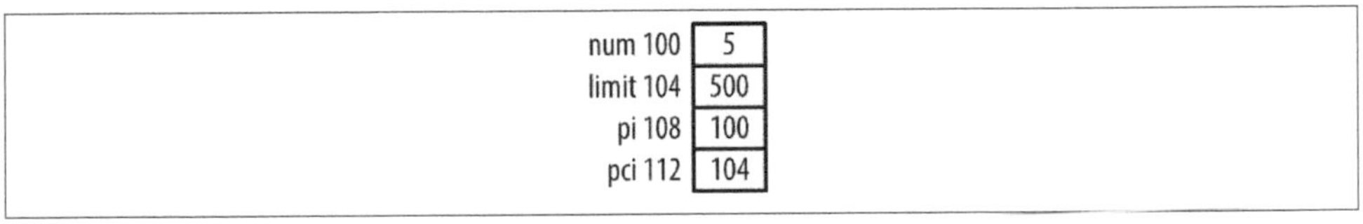

```
num 100   5
limit 104 500
pi 108    100
pci 112   104
```

Figure 1-11. Pointer to a constant integer

The following sequence will display the address and value of these variables:

```
printf("  num - Address: %p  value: %d\n",&num, num);
printf("limit - Address: %p  value: %d\n",&limit, limit);
printf("   pi - Address: %p  value: %p\n",&pi, pi);
printf("  pci - Address: %p  value: %p\n",&pci, pci);
```

When executed, this sequence will produce values similar to the following:

```
  num - Address: 100  value: 5
limit - Address: 104  value: 500
   pi - Address: 108  value: 100
  pci - Address: 112  value: 104
```

Dereferencing a constant pointer is fine if we are simply reading the integer's value. Reading is a perfectly legitimate and necessary capability, as shown below:

```
printf("%d\n", *pci);
```

We cannot dereference a constant pointer to change what the pointer references, but we can change the pointer. The pointer value is not constant. The pointer can be changed to reference another constant integer or a simple integer. Doing so will not be a problem. The declaration simply limits our ability to modify the referenced variable through the pointer.

This means the following assignment is legal:

```
pci = &num;
```

We can dereference pci to read it; however, we cannot dereference it to modify it.

Consider the following assignment:

```
*pci = 200;
```

This will result in the following syntax error:

```
'pci' : you cannot assign to a variable that is const
```

The pointer thinks it is pointing to a constant integer; therefore, it does not allow the modification of the integer using the pointer. We can still modify num using its name. We just can't use pci to modify it.

Conceptually, a constant pointer can also be visualized as shown in Figure 1-12. The clear boxes represent variables that can be changed. The shaded boxes represent variables that cannot be changed. The shaded box pointed to by pci cannot be changed using pci. The dashed line indicates that the pointer can reference that data type. In the previous example, pci pointed to limit.

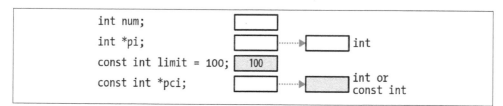

Figure 1-12. Pointer to a constant

The declaration of pci as a pointer to a constant integer means:

- pci can be assigned to point to different constant integers
- pci can be assigned to point to different nonconstant integers
- pci can be dereferenced for reading purposes
- pci cannot be dereferenced to change what it points to

The order of the type and the const keyword is not important. The following are equivalent:

```
const int *pci;
int const *pci;
```

Constant pointers to nonconstants

We can also declare a constant pointer to a nonconstant. When we do this, it means that while the pointer cannot be changed, the data pointed to can be modified. An example of such a pointer follows:

```
int num;
int *const cpi = &num;
```

With this declaration:

- cpi must be initialized to a nonconstant variable
- cpi cannot be modified
- The data pointed to by cpi can be modified

Conceptually, this type of pointer can be visualized as shown in Figure 1-13.

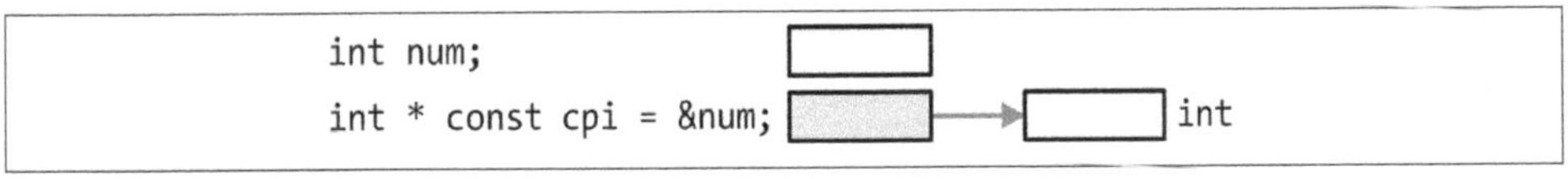

```
int num;

int * const cpi = &num;                    int
```

Figure 1-13. Constant pointers to nonconstants

It is possible to dereference cpi and assign a new value to whatever cpi is referencing. The following are two valid assignments:

```
*cpi = limit;
*cpi = 25;
```

However, if we attempt to initialize cpi to the constant limit as shown below, we will get a warning:

```
const int limit = 500;
int *const cpi = &limit;
```

The warning will appear as follows:

```
warning: initialization discards qualifiers from pointer target type
```

If cpi referenced the constant limit, the constant could be modified. This is not desirable. We generally prefer constants to remain constant.

Once an address has been assigned to cpi, we cannot assign a new value to cpi as shown below:

```
int num;
int age;
int *const cpi = &num;
cpi = &age;
```

The error message generated is shown below:

```
'cpi' : you cannot assign to a variable that is const
```

Constant pointers to constants

A constant pointer to a constant is an infrequently used pointer type. The pointer cannot be changed, and the data it points to cannot be changed through the pointer. An example of a constant pointer to a constant integer follows:

```
const int * const cpci = &limit;
```

A constant pointer to a constant can be visualized as shown in Figure 1-14.

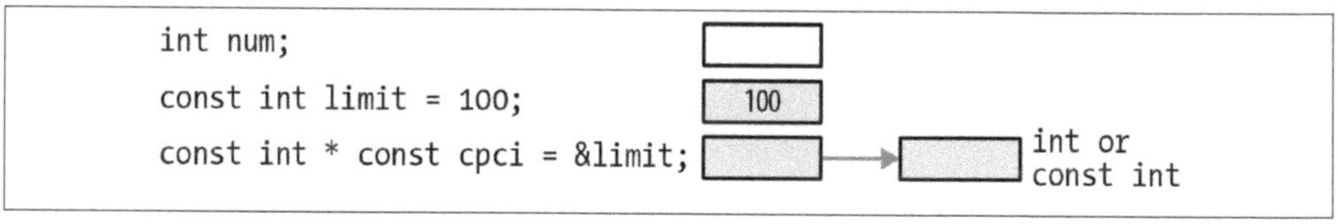

```
int num;

const int limit = 100;                    100

const int * const cpci = &limit;                          int or
                                                          const int
```

Figure 1-14. Constant pointers to constants

As with pointers to constants, it is not necessary to assign the address of a constant to cpci. Instead, we could have used num as shown below:

```
int num;
const int * const cpci = &num;
```

When the pointer is declared, we must initialize it. If we do not initialize it as shown below, we will get a syntax error:

```
const int * const cpci;
```

The syntax error will be similar to the following:

```
'cpci' : const object must be initialized if not extern
```

Given a constant pointer to a constant we cannot:

- Modify the pointer
- Modify the data pointed to by the pointer

Trying to assign a new address to cpci will result in a syntax error:

```
cpci = &num;
```

The syntax error follows:

```
'cpci' : you cannot assign to a variable that is const
```

If we try to dereference the pointer and assign a value as shown below, we will also get a syntax error:

```
*cpci = 25;
```

The error generated will be similar to the following:

```
'cpci' : you cannot assign to a variable that is const
expression must be a modifiable lvalue
```

Constant pointers to constants are rare.

Pointer to (constant pointer to constant)

Pointers to constants can also have multiple levels of indirection. In the following example, we declare a pointer to the cpci pointer explained in the previous section. Reading complex declarations from right to left helps clarify these types of declarations:

```
const int * const cpci = &limit;
const int * const * pcpci;
```

A pointer to a constant pointer to a constant can be visualized as shown in Figure 1-15.

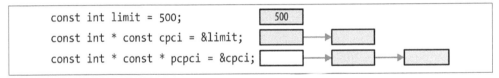

Figure 1-15. Pointer to (constant pointer to constant)

The following illustrates their use. The output of this sequence should display 500 twice:

```
printf("%d\n",*cpci);
pcpci = &cpci;
printf("%d\n",**pcpci);
```

The following table summarizes the first four types of pointers discussed in the previous sections:

Pointer Type	Pointer Modifiable	Data Pointed to Modifiable
Pointer to a nonconstant	✓	✓
Pointer to a constant	✓	X
Constant pointer to a nonconstant	X	✓
Constant pointer to a constant	X	X

Summary

In this chapter, we covered the essential aspects of pointers, including how to declare and use pointers in common situations. The interesting concept of null and its variations was covered, along with a number of pointer operators.

We found that the size of a pointer can vary, depending on the memory model supported by the target system and compiler. We also explored the use of the `const` keyword with pointers.

With this foundation, we are prepared to explore the other areas where pointers have proved to be quite useful. This includes their use as parameters to functions, in support of data structures, and in dynamically allocating memory. In addition, we will see the effect of their use in making applications more secure.

CHAPTER 2

Dynamic Memory Management in C

Much of the power of pointers stems from their ability to track dynamically allocated memory. The management of this memory through pointers forms the basis for many operations, including those used to manipulate complex data structures. To be able to fully exploit these capabilities, we need to understand how dynamic memory management occurs in C.

A C program executes within a *runtime system*. This is typically the environment provided by an operating system. The runtime system supports the stack and heap along with other program behavior.

Memory management is central to all programs. Sometimes memory is managed by the runtime system implicitly, such as when memory is allocated for automatic variables. In this case, variables are allocated to the enclosing function's stack frame. In the case of static and global variables, memory is placed in the application's data segment, where it is zeroed out. This is a separate area from executable code and other data managed by the runtime system.

The ability to allocate and then deallocate memory allows an application to manage its memory more efficiently and with greater flexibility. Instead of having to allocate memory to accommodate the largest possible size for a data structure, only the actual amount required needs to be allocated.

For example, arrays are fixed size in versions of C prior to C99. If we need to hold a variable number of elements, such as employee records, we would be forced to declare an array large enough to hold the maximum number of employees we believe would be needed. If we underestimate the size, we are forced to either recompile the application with a larger size or to take other approaches. If we overestimate the size, then we will waste space. The ability to dynamically allocate memory also helps when dealing with data structures using a variable number of elements, such as a linked list or a queue.

C99 introduced Variable Length Arrays (VLAs). The array's size is determined at runtime and not at compile time. However, once created, arrays still do not change size.

Languages such as C also support dynamic memory management where objects are allocated memory from the heap. This is done manually using functions to allocate and deallocate memory. The process is referred to as *dynamic memory management*.

We start this chapter with a quick overview of how memory is allocated and freed. Next, we present basic allocation functions such as malloc and realloc. The free function is discussed, including the use of NULL along with such problems as double free.

Dangling pointers are a common problem. We will present examples to illustrate when dangling pointers occur and techniques to handle the problem. The last section presents alternate techniques for managing memory. Improper use of pointers can result in unpredictable behavior. By this we mean the program can produce invalid results, corrupt data, or possibly terminate the program.

Dynamic Memory Allocation

The basic steps used for dynamic memory allocation in C are:

1. Use a malloc type function to allocate memory
2. Use this memory to support the application
3. Deallocate the memory using the free function

While there are some minor variations to this approach, this is the most common technique. In the following example, we allocate memory for an integer using the malloc function. The pointer assigns five to the allocated memory, and then the memory is released using the free function:

```
int *pi = (int*) malloc(sizeof(int));
*pi = 5;
printf("*pi: %d\n", *pi);
free(pi);
```

When this sequence is executed, it will display the number 5. Figure 2-1 illustrates how memory is allocated right before the free function is executed. For the purposes of this chapter, we will assume that the example code is found in the main function unless otherwise noted.

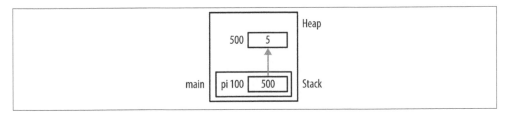

Figure 2-1. Allocating memory for an integer

The malloc function single argument specifies the number of bytes to allocate. If successful, it returns a pointer to memory allocated from the heap. If it fails, it returns a null pointer. Testing the validity of an allocated pointer is discussed in "Using the malloc Function". The sizeof operator makes the application more portable and determines the correct number of bytes to allocate for the host system.

In this example, we are trying to allocate enough memory for an integer. If we assume its size is 4, we can use:

```
int *pi = (int*) malloc(4));
```

However, the size of an integer can vary, depending on the memory model used. A portable approach is to use the sizeof operator. This will return the correct size regardless of where the program is executing.

A common error involving the dereference operator is demonstrated below:

```
int *pi;
*pi = (int*) malloc(sizeof(int));
```

The problem is with the lefthand side of the assignment operation. We are dereferencing the pointer. This will assign the address returned by malloc to the address stored in pi. If this is the first time an assignment is made to the pointer, then the address contained in the pointer is probably invalid. The correct approach is shown below:

```
pi = (int*) malloc(sizeof(int));
```

The dereference operator should not be used in this situation.

The free function, also discussed in more detail later, works in conjunction with malloc to deallocate the memory when it is no longer needed.

Each time the malloc function (or similar function) is called, a corresponding call to the free function must be made when the application is done with the memory to avoid memory leaks.

Once memory has been freed, it should not be accessed again. Normally, you would not intentionally access it after it had been deallocated. However, this can occur accidentally, as illustrated in the section "Dangling Pointers" on page 51. The system behaves in an implementation-dependent manner when this happens. A common practice is to always assign NULL to a freed pointer, as discussed in "Assigning NULL to a Freed Pointer" on page 48.

When memory is allocated, additional information is stored as part of a data structure maintained by the heap manager. This information includes, among other things, the block's size, and is typically placed immediately adjacent to the allocated block. If the application writes outside of this block of memory, then the data structure can be corrupted. This can lead to strange program behavior or corruption of the heap, as we will see in Chapter 7.

Consider the following code sequence. Memory is allocated for a string, allowing it to hold up to five characters plus the byte for the NUL termination character. The for loop writes zeros to each location but does not stop after writing six bytes. The for statement's terminal condition requires that it write eight bytes. The zeros being written are binary zeros and not the ASCII value for the character zero:

```
char *pc = (char*) malloc(6);
for(int i=0; i<8; i++) {
    *pc[i] = 0;
}
```

In Figure 2-2, extra memory has been allocated at the end of the six-byte string. This represents the extra memory used by the heap manager to keep track of the memory allocation. If we write past the end of the string, this extra memory will be corrupted. The extra memory is shown following the string in this example. However, its actual placement and its original content depend on the compiler.

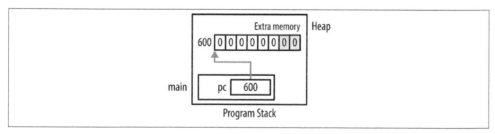

Figure 2-2. Extra memory used by heap manager

Memory Leaks

A memory leak occurs when allocated memory is never used again but is not freed. This can happen when:

- The memory's address is lost
- The free function is never invoked though it should be (sometimes called a hidden leak)

A problem with memory leaks is that the memory cannot be reclaimed and used later. The amount of memory available to the heap manager is decreased. If memory is repeatedly allocated and then lost, then the program may terminate when more memory is needed but malloc cannot allocate it because it ran out of memory. In extreme cases, the operating system may crash.

This is illustrated in the following simple example:

```
char *chunk;
while (1) {
    chunk = (char*) malloc(1000000);
    printf("Allocating\n");
}
```

The variable chunk is assigned memory from the heap. However, this memory is not freed before another block of memory is assigned to it. Eventually, the application will run out of memory and terminate abnormally. At minimum, memory is not being used efficiently.

Losing the address

An example of losing the address of memory is illustrated in the following code sequence where pi is reassigned a new address. The address of the first allocation of memory is lost when pi is allocated memory a second time.

```
int *pi = (int*) malloc(sizeof(int));
*pi = 5;
...
pi = (int*) malloc(sizeof(int));
```

This is illustrated in Figure 2-3 where the before and after images refer to the program's state before and after the second malloc's execution. The memory at address 500 has not been released, and the program no longer holds this address anywhere.

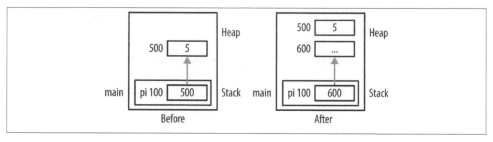

Figure 2-3. Losing an address

Another example allocates memory for a string, initializes it, and then displays the string character by character:

```c
char *name = (char*)malloc(strlen("Susan")+1);
strcpy(name,"Susan");
while(*name != 0) {
    printf("%c",*name);
    name++;
}
```

However, it increments `name` by one with each loop iteration. At the end, `name` is left pointing to the string's `NUL` termination character, as illustrated in Figure 2-4. The allocated memory's starting address has been lost.

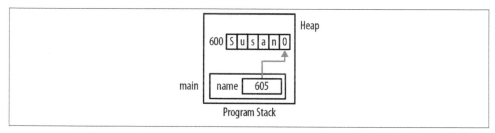

Figure 2-4. Losing address of dynamically allocated memory

Hidden memory leaks

Memory leaks can also occur when the program should release memory but does not. A hidden memory leak occurs when an object is kept in the heap even though the object is no longer needed. This is frequently the result of programmer oversight. The primary problem with this type of leak is that the object is using memory that is no longer needed and should be returned to the heap. In the worst case, the heap manager may not be able to allocate memory when requested, possibly forcing the program to terminate. At best, we are holding unneeded memory.

Memory leaks can also occur when freeing structures created using the `struct` keyword. If the structure contains pointers to dynamically allocated memory, then these pointers may need to be freed before the structure is freed. An example of this is found in Chapter 6.

Dynamic Memory Allocation Functions

Several memory allocation functions are available to manage dynamic memory. While what is available may be system dependent, the following functions are found on most systems in the *stdlib.h* header file:

- `malloc`
- `realloc`
- `calloc`
- `free`

The functions are summarized in Table 2-1.

Table 2-1. Dynamic memory allocation functions

Function	Description
malloc	Allocates memory from the heap
realloc	Reallocates memory to a larger or smaller amount based on a previously allocated block of memory
calloc	Allocates and zeros out memory from the heap
free	Returns a block of memory to the heap

Dynamic memory is allocated from the heap. With successive memory allocation calls, there is no guarantee regarding the order of the memory or the continuity of memory allocated. However, the memory allocated will be aligned according to the pointer's data type. For example, a four-byte integer would be allocated on an address boundary evenly divisible by four. The address returned by the heap manager will contain the lowest byte's address.

In Figure 2-3, the `malloc` function allocates four bytes at address 500. The second use of the `malloc` function allocates memory at address 600. They both are on four-byte address boundaries, and they did not allocate memory from consecutive memory locations.

Using the malloc Function

The function `malloc` allocates a block of memory from the heap. The number of bytes allocated is specified by its single argument. Its return type is a pointer to void. If memory is not available, `NULL` is returned. The function does not clear or otherwise modify the memory, thus the contents of memory should be treated as if it contained garbage. The function's prototype follows:

```
void* malloc(size_t);
```

The function possesses a single argument of type `size_t`. This type is discussed in Chapter 1. You need to be careful when passing variables to this function, as problems can arise if the argument is a negative number. On some systems, a NULL value is returned if the argument is negative.

When `malloc` is used with an argument of zero, its behavior is implementation-specific. It may return a pointer to NULL or it may return a pointer to a region with zero bytes allocated. If the `malloc` function is used with a NULL argument, then it will normally generate a warning and execute returning zero bytes.

The following shows a typical use of the `malloc` function:

```
int *pi = (int*) malloc(sizeof(int));
```

The following steps are performed when the `malloc` function is executed:

1. Memory is allocated from the heap
2. The memory is *not* modified or otherwise cleared
3. The first byte's address is returned

 Since the `malloc` function may return a NULL value if it is unable to allocate memory, it is a good practice to check for a NULL value before using the pointer as follows:

```
int *pi = (int*) malloc(sizeof(int));
if(pi != NULL) {
    // Pointer should be good
} else {
    // Bad pointer
}
```

To cast or not to cast

Before the pointer to void was introduced to C, explicit casts were required with `malloc` to stop the generation of warnings when assignments were made between incompatible pointer types. Since a pointer to void can be assigned to any other pointer type, explicit casting is no longer required. Some developers consider explicit casts to be a good practice because:

- They document the intention of the `malloc` function
- They make the code compatible with C++ (or earlier C compiler), which require explicit casts

Using casts will be a problem if you fail to include the header file for malloc. The compiler may generate warnings. By default, C assumes functions return an integer. If you fail to include a prototype for malloc, it will complain when you try to assign an integer to a pointer.

Failing to allocate memory

If you declare a pointer but fail to allocate memory to the address it points to before using it, that memory will usually contain garbage, resulting typically in an invalid memory reference. Consider the following code sequence:

```
int *pi;
...
printf("%d\n",*pi);
```

The allocation of memory is shown in Figure 2-5. This issue is covered in more detail in Chapter 7.

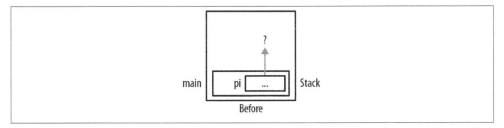

Figure 2-5. Failure to allocate memory

When executed, this can result in a runtime exception. This type of problem is common with strings, as shown below:

```
char *name;
printf("Enter a name: ");
scanf("%s",name);
```

While it may seem like this would execute correctly, we are using memory referenced by name. However, this memory has not been allocated. This problem can be illustrated graphically by changing the variable, pi, in Figure 2-5 to name.

Not using the right size for the malloc function

The malloc function allocates the number of bytes specified by its argument. You need to be careful when using the function to allocate the correct number of bytes. For example, if we want to allocate space for 10 doubles, then we need to allocate 80 bytes. This is achieved as shown below:

```
double *pd = (double*)malloc(NUMBER_OF_DOUBLES * sizeof(double));
```

Use the sizeof operator when specifying the number of bytes to allocate for data types whenever possible.

In the following example, an attempt is made to allocate memory for 10 doubles:

```c
const int NUMBER_OF_DOUBLES = 10;
double *pd = (double*)malloc(NUMBER_OF_DOUBLES);
```

However, the code only allocated 10 bytes.

Determining the amount of memory allocated

There is no standard way to determine the total amount of memory allocated by the heap. However, some compilers provide extensions for this purpose. In addition, there is no standard way of determining the size of a memory block allocated by the heap manager.

For example, if we allocate 64 bytes for a string, the heap manager will allocate additional memory to manage this block. The total size allocated, and the amount used by the heap manager, is the sum of these two quantities. This was illustrated in Figure 2-2.

The maximum size that can be allocated with malloc is system dependent. It would seem like this size should be limited by size_t. However, limitations can be imposed by the amount of physical memory present and other operating system constraints.

When malloc executes, it is supposed to allocate the amount of memory requested and then return the memory's address. What happens if the underlying operating system uses "lazy initialization" where it does not actually allocate the memory until it is accessed? A problem can arise at this point if there is not enough memory available to allocate. The answer depends on the runtime and operating systems. A typical developer normally would not need to deal with this question because such initialization schemes are quite rare.

Using malloc with static and global pointers

You cannot use a function call when initializing a static or global variable. In the following code sequence, we declare a static variable and then attempt to initialize it using malloc:

```c
static int *pi = malloc(sizeof(int));
```

This will generate a compile-time error message. The same thing happens with global variables but can be avoided for static variables by using a separate statement to allocate memory to the variable as follows. We cannot use a separate assignment statement with global variables because global variables are declared outside of a function and executable code, such as the assignment statement, must be inside of a function:

```
static int *pi;
pi = malloc(sizeof(int));
```

 From the compiler standpoint, there is a difference between using the initialization operator, =, and using the assignment operator, =.

Using the calloc Function

The `calloc` function will allocate and clear memory at the same time. Its prototype follows:

```
void *calloc(size_t numElements, size_t elementSize);
```

 To clear memory means its contents are set to all binary zeros.

The function will allocate memory determined by the product of the `numElements` and `elementSize` parameters. A pointer is returned to the first byte of memory. If the function is unable to allocate memory, `NULL` is returned. Originally, this function was used to aid in the allocation of memory for arrays.

If either `numElements` or `elementSize` is zero, then a null pointer may be returned. If `calloc` is unable to allocate memory, a null pointer is returned and the global variable, `errno`, is set to `ENOMEM` (out of memory). This is a `POSIX` error code and may not be available on all systems.

Consider the following example where `pi` is allocated a total of 20 bytes, all containing zeros:

```
int *pi = calloc(5,sizeof(int));
```

Instead of using `calloc`, the `malloc` function along with the `memset` function can be used to achieve the same results, as shown below:

```
int *pi = malloc(5 * sizeof(int));
memset(pi, 0, 5* sizeof(int));
```

 The `memset` function will fill a block with a value. The first argument is a pointer to the buffer to fill. The second is the value used to fill the buffer, and the last argument is the number of bytes to be set.

Use `calloc` when memory needs to be zeroed out. However, the execution of `calloc` may take longer than using `malloc`.

 The function `cfree` is no longer needed. In the early days of C it was used to free memory allocated by `calloc`.

Using the realloc Function

Periodically, it may be necessary to increase or decrease the amount of memory allocated to a pointer. This is particularly useful when a variable size array is needed, as will be demonstrated in Chapter 4. The `realloc` function will reallocate memory. Its prototype follows:

```
void *realloc(void *ptr, size_t size);
```

The function `realloc` returns a pointer to a block of memory. The function takes two arguments. The first is a pointer to the original block, and the second is the requested size. The reallocated block's size will be different from the size of the block referenced by the first argument. The return value is a pointer to the reallocated memory.

The requested size may be smaller or larger than the currently allocated amount. If the size is less than what is currently allocated, then the excess memory is returned to the heap. There is no guarantee that the excess memory will be cleared. If the size is greater than what is currently allocated, then if possible, the memory will be allocated from the region immediately following the current allocation. Otherwise, memory is allocated from a different region of the heap and the old memory is copied to the new region.

If the size is zero and the pointer is not null, then the pointer will be freed. If space cannot be allocated, then the original block of memory is retained and is not changed. However, the pointer returned is a null pointer and the `errno` is set to `ENOMEM`.

The function's behavior is summarized in Table 2-2.

Table 2-2. Behavior of realloc function

First Parameter	Second Parameter	Behavior
null	NA	Same as `malloc`
Not null	0	Original block is freed
Not null	Less than the original block's size	A smaller block is allocated using the current block
Not null	Larger than the original block's size	A larger block is allocated either from the current location or another region of the heap

In the following example, we use two variables to allocate memory for a string. Initially, we allocate 16 bytes but only use the first 13 bytes (12 hexadecimal digits and the null termination character (0)):

```
char *string1;
char *string2;
string1 = (char*) malloc(16);
strcpy(string1, "0123456789AB");
```

Next, we use the `realloc` function to specify a smaller region of memory. The address and contents of these two variables are then displayed:

```
string2 = realloc(string1, 8);
printf("string1  Value: %p [%s]\n", string1, string1);
printf("string2  Value: %p [%s]\n", string2, string2);
```

The output follows:

```
string1  Value: 0x500 [0123456789AB]
string2  Value: 0x500 [0123456789AB]
```

The allocation of memory is illustrated in Figure 2-6.

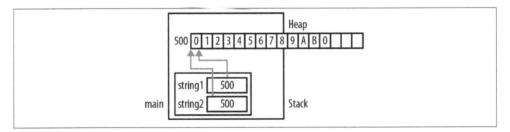

Figure 2-6. realloc example

The heap manager was able to reuse the original block, and it did not modify its contents. However, the program continued to use more than the eight bytes requested. That is, we did not change the string to fit into the eight-byte block. In this example, we should have adjusted the length of the string so that it fits into the eight reallocated bytes. The simplest way of doing this is to assign a NUL character to address 507. Using more space than allocated is not a good practice and should be avoided, as detailed in Chapter 7.

In this next example, we will reallocate additional memory:

```
string1 = (char*) malloc(16);
strcpy(string1, "0123456789AB");
string2 = realloc(string1, 64);
printf("string1  Value: %p [%s]\n", string1, string1);
printf("string2  Value: %p [%s]\n", string2, string2);
```

When executed, you may get results similar to the following:

```
string1  Value: 0x500 [0123456789AB]
string2  Value: 0x600 [0123456789AB]
```

In this example, `realloc` had to allocate a new block of memory. Figure 2-7 illustrates the allocation of memory.

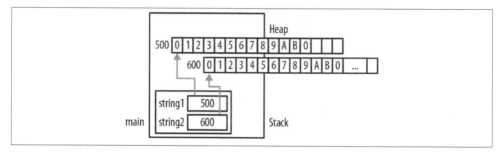

Figure 2-7. Allocating additional memory

The alloca Function and Variable Length Arrays

The `alloca` function (Microsoft's `malloca`) allocates memory by placing it in the stack frame for the function. When the function returns, the memory is automatically freed. This function can be difficult to implement if the underlying runtime system is not stack-based. As a result, this function is nonstandard and should be avoided if the application needs to be portable.

In C99, Variable Length Arrays (VLAs) were introduced, allowing the declaration and creation of an array within a function whose size is based on a variable. In the following example, an array of `char` is allocated for use in a function:

```
void compute(int size) {
    char buffer[size];
    ...
}
```

This means the allocation of memory is done at runtime and memory is allocated as part of the stack frame. Also, when the `sizeof` operator is used with the array, it will be executed at runtime rather than compile time.

A small runtime penalty will be imposed. Also, when the function exits, the memory is effectively deallocated. Since we did not use a `malloc` type function to create it, we should not use the `free` function to deallocate it. The function should not return a pointer to this memory either. This issue is addressed in Chapter 5.

VLAs do not change size. Their size is fixed once they are allocated. If you need an array whose size actually changes, then an approach such as using the realloc function, as discussed in the section "Using the realloc Function" on page 44, is needed.

Deallocating Memory Using the free Function

With dynamic memory allocation, the programmer is able to return memory when it is no longer being used, thus freeing it up for other uses. This is normally performed using the free function, whose prototype is shown below:

```
void free(void *ptr);
```

The pointer argument should contain the address of memory allocated by a malloc type function. This memory is returned to the heap. While the pointer may still point to the region, always assume it points to garbage. This region may be reallocated later and populated with different data.

In the simple example below, pi is allocated memory and is eventually freed:

```
int *pi = (int*) malloc(sizeof(int));
...
free(pi);
```

Figure 2-8 illustrates the allocation of memory immediately before and right after the free function executes. The dashed box at address 500 that indicates the memory has been freed but still may contain its value. The variable pi still contains the address 500. This is called a dangling pointer and is discussed in detail in the section "Dangling Pointers" on page 51.

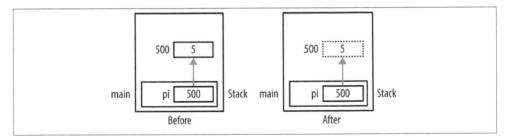

Figure 2-8. Release of memory using free

If the free function is passed a null pointer, then it normally does nothing. If the pointer passed has been allocated by other than a malloc type function, then the function's behavior is undefined. In the following example, pi is allocated the address of num. However, this is not a valid heap address:

```
int num;
int *pi = &num;
free(pi);  // Undefined behavior
```

 Manage memory allocation/deallocation at the same level. For example, if a pointer is allocated within a function, deallocate it in the same function.

Assigning NULL to a Freed Pointer

Pointers can cause problems even after they have been freed. If we try to dereference a freed pointer, its behavior is undefined. As a result, some programmers will explicitly assign NULL to a pointer to designate the pointer as invalid. Subsequent use of such a pointer will result in a runtime exception.

An example of this approach follows:

```
int *pi = (int*) malloc(sizeof(int));
...
free(pi);
pi = NULL;
```

The allocation of memory is illustrated in Figure 2-9.

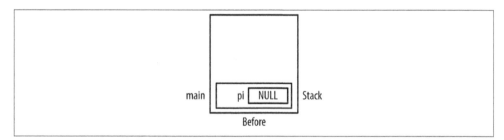

Figure 2-9. Assigning NULL after using free

This technique attempts to address problems like dangling pointers. However, it is better to spend time addressing the conditions that caused the problems rather than crudely catching them with a null pointer. In addition, you cannot assign NULL to a constant pointer except when it is initialized.

Double Free

The term *double free* refers to an attempt to free a block of memory twice. A simple example follows:

```
int *pi = (int*) malloc(sizeof(int));
*pi = 5;
free(pi);
...
free(pi);
```

The execution of the second free function will result in a runtime exception. A less obvious example involves the use of two pointers, both pointing to the same block of memory. As shown below, the same runtime exception will result when we accidentally try to free the same memory a second time:

```
p1 = (int*) malloc(sizeof(int));
int *p2 = p1;
free(p1);
...
free(p2);
```

This allocation of memory is illustrated in Figure 2-10.

 When two pointers reference the same location, it is referred to as *aliasing*. This concept is discussed in Chapter 8.

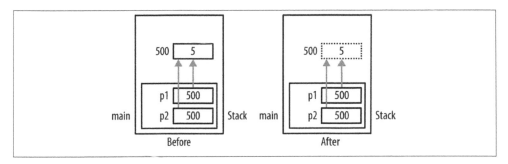

Figure 2-10. Double free

Unfortunately, heap managers have a difficult time determining whether a block has already been deallocated. Thus, they don't attempt to detect the same memory being freed twice. This normally results in a corrupt heap and program termination. Even if the program does not terminate, it represents questionable problem logic. There is no reason to free the same memory twice.

It has been suggested that the free function should assign a NULL or some other special value to its argument when it returns. However, since pointers are passed by value, the free function is unable to explicitly assign NULL to the pointer. This is explained in more detail in the section "Passing a Pointer to a Pointer" on page 68.

The Heap and System Memory

The heap typically uses operating system functions to manage its memory. The heap's size may be fixed when the program is created, or it may be allowed to grow. However, the heap manager does not necessarily return memory to the operating system when the free function is called. The deallocated memory is simply made available for subsequent use by the application. Thus, when a program allocates and then frees up memory, the deallocation of memory is not normally reflected in the application's memory usage as seen from the operating system perspective.

Freeing Memory upon Program Termination

The operating system is responsible for maintaining the resources of an application, including its memory. When an application terminates, it is the operating system's responsibility to reallocate this memory for other applications. The state of the terminated application's memory, corrupted or uncorrupted, is not an issue. In fact, one of the reasons an application may terminate is because its memory is corrupted. With an abnormal program termination, cleanup may not be possible. Thus, there is no reason to free allocated memory before the application terminates.

With this said, there may be other reasons why this memory should be freed. The conscientious programmer may want to free memory as a quality issue. It is always a good habit to free memory after it is no longer needed, even if the application is terminating. If you use a tool to detect memory leaks or similar problems, then deallocating memory will clean up the output of such tools. In some less complex operating systems, the operating system may not reclaim memory automatically, and it may be the program's responsibility to reclaim memory before terminating. Also, a later version of the application could add code toward the end of the program. If the previous memory has not been freed, problems could arise.

Thus, ensuring that all memory is free before program termination:

- May be more trouble than it's worth
- Can be time consuming and complicated for the deallocation of complex structures
- Can add to the application's size
- Results in longer running time
- Introduces the opportunity for more programming errors

Whether memory should be deallocated prior to program termination is application-specific.

Dangling Pointers

If a pointer still references the original memory after it has been freed, it is called a dangling pointer. The pointer does not point to a valid object. This is sometimes referred to as a premature free.

The use of dangling pointers can result in a number of different types of problems, including:

- Unpredictable behavior if the memory is accessed
- *Segmentation faults* when the memory is no longer accessible
- Potential security risks

These types of problems can result when:

- Memory is accessed after it has been freed
- A pointer is returned to an automatic variable in a previous function call (discussed in the section "Pointers to Local Data" on page 66)

Dangling Pointer Examples

Below is a simple example where we allocate memory for an integer using the malloc function. Next, the memory is released using the free function:

```
int *pi = (int*) malloc(sizeof(int));
*pi = 5;
printf("*pi: %d\n", *pi);
free(pi);
```

The variable pi will still hold the integer's address. However, this memory may be reused by the heap manager and may hold data other than an integer. Figure 2-11 illustrates the program's state immediately before and after the free function is executed. The pi variable is assumed to be part of the main function and is located at address 100. The memory allocated using malloc is found at address 500.

When the free function is executed, the memory at address 500 has been deallocated and should not be used. However, most runtime systems will not prevent subsequent access or modification. We may still attempt to write to the location as shown below. The result of this action is unpredictable.

```
free(pi);
*pi = 10;
```

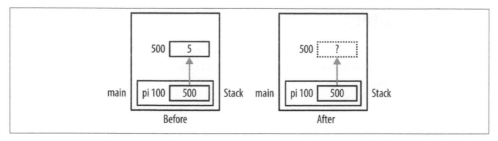

Figure 2-11. Dangling pointer

A more insidious example occurs when more than one pointer references the same area of memory and one of them is freed. As shown below, p1 and p2 both refer to the same area of memory, which is called pointer aliasing. However, p1 is freed:

```
int *p1 = (int*) malloc(sizeof(int));
*p1 = 5;
...
int *p2;
p2 = p1;
...
free(p1);
...
*p2 = 10;    // Dangling pointer
```

Figure 2-12 illustrates the allocation of memory where the dotted box represents freed memory.

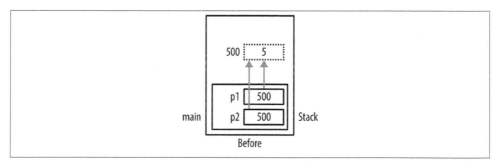

Figure 2-12. Dangling pointer with aliased pointers

A subtle problem can occur when using block statements, as shown below. Here pi is assigned the address of tmp. The variable pi may be a global variable or a local variable. However, when tmp's enclosing block is popped off of the program stack, the address is no longer valid:

```
int *pi;
...
```

```
{
    int tmp = 5;
    pi = &tmp;
}
// pi is now a dangling pointer
foo();
```

Most compilers will treat a block statement as a stack frame. The variable tmp was allocated on the stack frame and subsequently popped off the stack when the block statement was exited. The pointer pi is now left pointing to a region of memory that may eventually be overridden by a different activation record, such as the function foo. This condition is illustrated in Figure 2-13.

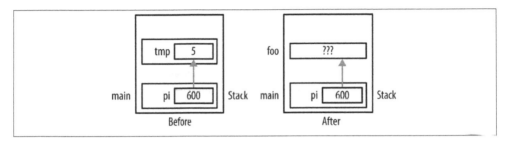

Figure 2-13. Block statement problem

Dealing with Dangling Pointers

Debugging pointer-induced problems can be difficult to resolve at times. Several approaches exist for dealing with dangling pointers, including:

- Setting a pointer to NULL after freeing it. Its subsequent use will terminate the application. However, problems can still persist if multiple copies of the pointer exist. This is because the assignment will only affect one of the copies, as illustrated in the section "Double Free" on page 48.

- Writing special functions to replace the free function (see "Writing your own free function" on page 70).

- Some systems (runtime/debugger) will overwrite data when it is freed (e.g., 0xDEADBEEF - Visual Studio will use 0xCC, 0xCD, or 0xDD, depending on what is freed). While no exceptions are thrown, when the programmer sees memory containing these values where they are not expected, he knows that the program may be accessing freed memory.

- Use third-party tools to detect dangling pointers and other problems.

Displaying pointer values can be helpful in debugging dangling pointers, but you need to be careful how they are displayed. We have already discussed how to display pointer values in "Displaying Pointer Values" on page 9. Make sure you display them consistently to avoid confusion when comparing pointer values. The assert macro can also be useful, as demonstrated in "Dealing with Uninitialized Pointers" on page 162.

Debug Version Support for Detecting Memory Leaks

Microsoft provides techniques for addressing overwriting of dynamically allocated memory and memory leaks. This approach uses special memory management techniques in debug versions of a program to:

- Check the heap's integrity
- Check for memory leaks
- Simulate low heap memory situations

Microsoft does this by using a special data structure to manage memory allocation. This structure maintains debug information, such as the filename and line number where malloc is called. In addition, buffers are allocated before and after the actual memory allocation to detect overwriting of the actual memory. More information about this technique can be found at Microsoft Developer Network (*http://bit.ly/12SftWV*).

The Mudflap Libraries (*http://bit.ly/YilPI1*) provide a similar capability for the GCC compiler. Its runtime library supports the detection of memory leaks, among other things. This detection is accomplished by instrumenting the pointer dereferencing operations.

Dynamic Memory Allocation Technologies

So far, we have talked about the heap manager's allocating and deallocating memory. However, the implementation of this technology can vary by compiler. Most heap managers use a heap or data segment as the source for memory. However, this approach is subject to fragmentation and may collide with the program stack. Nevertheless, it is the most common way of implementing the heap.

Heap managers need to address many issues, such as whether heaps are allocated on a per process and/or per thread basis and how to protect the heap from security breaches.

There are a number of heap managers, including OpenBSD's malloc, Hoard's malloc, and TCMalloc developed by Google. The GNU C library allocator is based on the general-purpose allocator dlmalloc (*http://dmalloc.com/*). It provides facilities for debugging and can help in tracking memory leaks. The dlmalloc's logging feature tracks memory usage and memory transaction, among other actions.

A manual technique for managing the memory used for structures is presented in "Avoiding malloc/free Overhead" on page 139.

Garbage Collection in C

The `malloc` and `free` functions provide a way of manually allocating and deallocating memory. However, there are numerous issues regarding the use of manual memory management in C, such as performance, achieving good locality of reference, threading problems, and cleaning up memory gracefully.

Several nonstandard techniques can be used to address some of these issues, and this section explores some of them. A key feature of these techniques is the automatic deallocation of memory. When memory is no longer needed, it is collected and made available for use later in the program. The deallocated memory is referred to as garbage. Hence, the term *garbage collection* denotes the processing of this memory.

Garbage collection is useful for a number of reasons, including:

- Freeing the programmer from having to decide when to deallocate memory
- Allowing the programmer to focus on the application's problem

One alternative to manual memory management is the Boehm-Weiser Collector (*http://www.hpl.hp.com/personal/Hans_Boehm/gc/*). However, this is not part of the language.

Resource Acquisition Is Initialization

Resource Acquisition Is Initialization (RAII) is a technique invented by Bjarne Stroustrup. It addresses the allocation and deallocation of resources in C++. The technique is useful for guaranteeing the allocation and subsequent deallocation of a resource in the presence of exceptions. Allocated resources will eventually be released.

There have been several approaches for using RAII in C. The GNU compiler provides a nonstandard extension to support this. We will illustrate this extension by showing how memory can be allocated and then freed within a function. When the variable goes out of scope, the deallocation process occurs automatically.

The GNU extension uses a macro called `RAII_VARIABLE`. It declares a variable and associates with the variable:

- A type
- A function to execute when the variable is created
- A function to execute when the variable goes out of scope

The macro is shown below:

```
#define RAII_VARIABLE(vartype,varname,initval,dtor) \
    void _dtor_ ## varname (vartype * v) { dtor(*v); } \
    vartype varname __attribute__((cleanup(_dtor_ ## varname))) = (initval)
```

In the following example, we declare a variable called `name` as a pointer to `char`. When it is created, the `malloc` function is executed, allocating 32 bytes to it. When the function is terminated, `name` goes out of scope and the `free` function is executed:

```
void raiiExample() {
    RAII_VARIABLE(char*, name, (char*)malloc(32), free);
    strcpy(name,"RAII Example");
    printf("%s\n",name);
}
```

When this function is executed, the string "RAII_Example" will be displayed.

Similar results can be achieved (*http://bit.ly/ZwR5Sx*) without using the GNU extension.

Using Exception Handlers

Another approach to deal with the deallocation of memory is to use exception handling (*http://bit.ly/13vn8He*). While exception handling is not a standard part of C, it can be useful if available and possible portability issues are not a concern. The following illustrates the approach using the Microsoft Visual Studio version of the C language.

Here the try block encloses any statements that might cause an exception to be thrown at runtime. The finally block will be executed regardless of whether an exception is thrown. The `free` function is guaranteed to be executed.

```
void exceptionExample() {
    int *pi = NULL;
    __try {
        pi = (int*)malloc(sizeof(int));
        *pi = 5;
        printf("%d\n",*pi);
    }
    __finally {
        free(pi);
    }
}
```

You can implement exception handling in C using several other approaches.

Summary

Dynamic memory allocation is a significant C language feature. In this chapter, we focused on the manual allocation of memory using the `malloc` and `free` functions. We addressed a number of common problems involving these functions, including the failure to allocate memory and dangling pointers.

There are other nonstandard techniques for managing dynamic memory in C. We touched on a few of these garbage collection techniques, including RAII and exception handling.

CHAPTER 3

Pointers and Functions

Pointers contribute immensely to a function's capability. They allow data to be passed and modified by a function. Complex data can also be passed and returned from a function in the form of a pointer to a structure. When pointers hold the address of a function, they provide a means to dynamically control a program's execution flow. In this chapter, we will explore the power of pointers as used with functions and learn how to use them to solve many real-world problems.

To understand functions and their use with pointers, a good understanding of the program stack is needed. The program stack is used by most modern block-structured languages, such as C, to support the execution of functions. When a function is invoked, its stack frame is created and then pushed onto the program stack. When the function returns, its stack frame is popped off of the program stack.

When working with functions, there are two areas where pointers become useful. The first is when we pass a pointer to a function. This allows the function to modify data referenced by the pointer and to pass blocks of information more efficiently.

The second area is declaring a pointer to a function. In essence, function notation is pointer notation. The function's name evaluates to the address of the function, and the function's parameters are passed to the function. As we will see, function pointers provide additional capability to control the execution flow of a program.

In this section, we will establish the foundation for understanding and working with functions and pointers. Because of the pervasiveness of functions and pointers, this foundation should serve you well.

Program Stack and Heap

The program stack and the heap are important runtime elements of C. In this section, we will carefully examine the structure and use of the program stack and heap. We will also look at the stack frame's structure, which holds local variables.

 Local variables are also called automatic variables. They are always allocated to a stack frame.

Program Stack

The program stack is an area of memory that supports the execution of functions and is normally shared with the heap. That is, they share the same region of memory. The program stack tends to occupy the lower part of this region, while the heap uses the upper part.

The program stack holds *stack frames*, sometimes called *activation records* or *activation frames*. Stack frames hold the parameters and local variables of a function. The heap manages dynamic memory and is discussed in "Dynamic Memory Allocation" on page 34.

Figure 3-1 illustrates how the stack and heap are organized conceptually. This illustration is based on the following code sequence:

```
void function2() {
    Object *var1 = ...;
    int var2;
    printf("Program Stack Example\n");
}

void function1() {
    Object *var3 = ...;
    function2();
}

int main() {
    int var4;
    function1();
}
```

As functions are called, their stack frames are pushed onto the stack and the stack grows "upward." When a function terminates, its stack frame is popped off the program stack. The memory used by the stack frame is not cleared and may eventually be overridden by another stack frame when it is pushed onto the program stack.

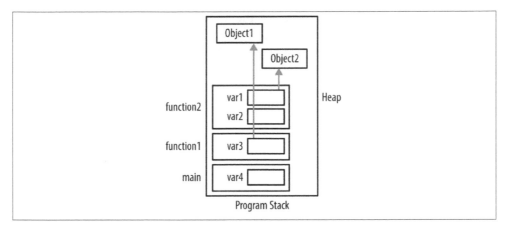

Figure 3-1. Stack and heap

When memory is dynamically allocated, it comes from the heap, which tends to grow "downward." The heap will fragment as memory is allocated and then deallocated. Although the heap tends to grow downward, this is a general direction. Memory can be allocated from anywhere within the heap.

Organization of a Stack Frame

A stack frame consists of several elements, including:

Return address
    The address in the program where the function is to return upon completion

Storage for local data
    Memory allocated for local variables

Storage for parameters
    Memory allocated for the function's parameters

Stack and base pointers
    Pointers used by the runtime system to manage the stack

The typical C programmer will not be concerned about the stack and base pointers used in support of a stack frame. However, understanding what they are and how they are used provides a more in-depth understanding of the program stack.

A stack pointer usually points to the top of the stack. A stack base pointer (frame pointer) is often present and points to an address within the stack frame, such as the return address. This pointer assists in accessing the stack frame's elements. Neither of these pointers are C pointers. They are addresses used by the runtime system to manage the program stack. If the runtime system is implemented in C, then these pointers may be real C pointers.

Consider the creation of a stack frame for the following function. This function has passed an array of integers and an integer representing the array's size. Three `printf` statements are used to display the parameter's and the local variable's addresses:

```c
float average(int *arr, int size) {
    int sum;
    printf("arr: %p\n",&arr);
    printf("size: %p\n",&size);
    printf("sum: %p\n",&sum);

    for(int i=0; i<size; i++) {
        sum += arr[i];
    }
    return (sum * 1.0f) / size;
}
```

When executed, you get output similar to the following:

```
arr: 0x500
size: 0x504
sum: 0x480
```

The gap in the addresses between the parameters and the local variables is due to other elements of the stack frame used by the runtime system to manage the stack.

When the stack frame is created, the parameters are pushed onto the frame in the opposite order of their declaration, followed by the local variables. This is illustrated in Figure 3-2. In this case, `size` is pushed followed by `arr`. Typically, the return address for the function call is pushed next, followed by the local variables. They are pushed in the opposite order in which they were listed.

Conceptually, the stack in this example grows "up." However, the stack frame's parameters and local variables and new stack frames are added at lower memory addresses. The actual direction the stack grows is implementation-specific.

The variable `i` used in the `for` statement is not included as part of this stack frame. C treats block statements as "mini" functions and will push and pop them as appropriate. In this case, the block statement is pushed onto the program stack above the `average` stack frame when it is executed and then popped off when it is done.

While the precise addresses can vary, the order usually will not. This is important to understand, as it helps explain how memory is allocated and establishes the relative order of the parameters and variables. This can be useful when debugging pointer problems. If you are not aware of how the stack frame is allocated, the assignment of addresses may not make sense.

As stack frames are pushed onto the program stack, the system may run out of memory. This condition is called stack overflow and generally results in the program terminating abnormally. Keep in mind that each thread is typically allocated its own program stack.

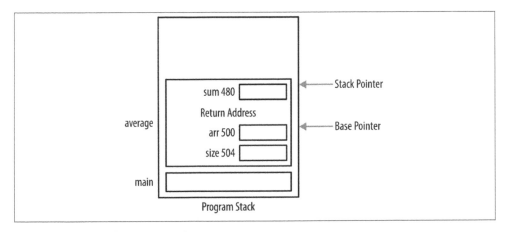

Figure 3-2. Stack frame example

This can lead to potential conflicts if one or more threads access the same object in memory. This will be addressed in "Sharing Pointers Between Threads" on page 186.

Passing and Returning by Pointer

In this section, we will examine the impact of passing and returning pointers to and from functions. Passing pointers allows the referenced object to be accessible in multiple functions without making the object global. This means that only those functions that need access to the object will get this access and that the object does not need to be duplicated.

If the data needs to be modified in a function, it needs to be passed by pointer. We can pass data by pointer and prohibit it from being modified by passing it as a pointer to a constant, as will be demonstrated in the section "Passing a Pointer to a Constant" on page 63. When the data is a pointer that needs to be modified, then we pass it as a pointer to a pointer. This topic is covered in "Passing a Pointer to a Pointer" on page 68.

Parameters, including pointers, are passed by value. That is, a copy of the argument is passed to the function. Passing a pointer to an argument can be efficient when dealing with large data structures. For example, consider a large structure that represents an employee. If we passed the entire structure to the function, then every byte of the structure would need to be copied, resulting in a slower program and in more space being used in the stack frame. Passing a pointer to the object means the object does not have to be copied, and we can access the object through the pointer.

Passing Data Using a Pointer

One of the primary reasons for passing data using a pointer is to allow the function to modify the data. The following sequence implements a swap function that will interchange the values referenced by its parameters. This is a common operation found in a number of sorting algorithms. Here, we use integer pointers and dereference them to affect the swap operation:

```
void swapWithPointers(int* pnum1, int* pnum2) {
    int tmp;
    tmp = *pnum1;
    *pnum1 = *pnum2;
    *pnum2 = tmp;
}
```

The following code sequence demonstrates this function:

```
int main() {
    int n1 = 5;
    int n2 = 10;
    swapWithPointers(&n1, &n2);
    return 0;
}
```

The pointers pnum1 and pnum2 are dereferenced during the swap operation. This will result in the values of n1 and n2 being modified. Figure 3-3 illustrates how memory is organized. The Before image shows the program stack at the beginning of the swap function, and the After image shows it just before the function returns.

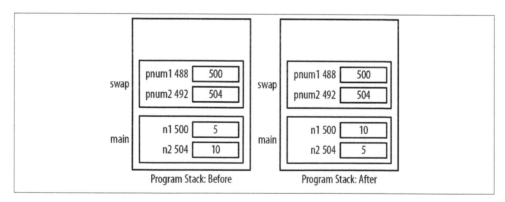

Figure 3-3. Swapping with pointers

Passing Data by Value

If we do not pass them by pointers, then the swap operation will not occur. In the following function, the two integers are passed by value:

```
void swap(int num1, int num2) {
    int tmp;
    tmp = num1;
    num1 = num2;
    num2 = tmp;
}
```

In the following code sequence, two integers are passed to the function:

```
int main() {
    int n1 = 5;
    int n2 = 10;
    swap(n1, n2);
    return 0;
}
```

However, this will not work because the integers were passed by value and not by pointer. Only a copy of the arguments is stored in num1 and num2. If we modify num1, then the argument n1 is not changed. When we modify the parameters, we are not modifying the original arguments. Figure 3-4 illustrates how memory is allocated for the parameters.

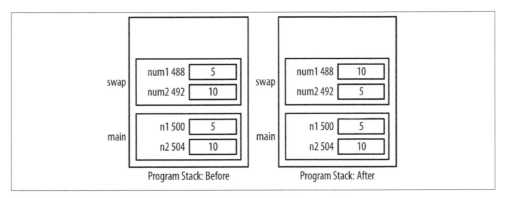

Figure 3-4. Pass by value

Passing a Pointer to a Constant

Passing a pointer to constant is a common technique used in C. It is efficient, as we are only passing the address of the data and can avoid copying large amounts of memory in some cases. However, with a simple pointer, the data can be modified. When this is not desirable, then passing a pointer to a constant is the answer.

In this example, we pass a pointer to a constant integer and a pointer to an integer. Within the function, we cannot modify the value passed as a pointer to a constant:

```
void passingAddressOfConstants(const int* num1, int* num2) {
    *num2 = *num1;
}
```

```
int main() {
    const int limit = 100;
    int result = 5;
    passingAddressOfConstants(&limit, &result);
    return 0;
}
```

No syntax errors will be generated, and the function will assign 100 to the variable result. In the following version of the function, we attempt to modify both referenced integers:

```
void passingAddressOfConstants(const int* num1, int* num2) {
    *num1 = 100;
    *num2 = 200;
}
```

This will cause a problem if we pass the constant limit to the function twice:

```
const int limit = 100;
passingAddressOfConstants(&limit, &limit);
```

This will generate syntax errors that complain of a type mismatch between the second parameter and its argument. In addition, it will complain that we are attempting to modify the presumed constant referenced by the first parameter.

The function expected a pointer to an integer, but a pointer to an integer constant was passed instead. We cannot pass the address of an integer constant to a pointer to an integer, as this would allow a constant value to be modified. This is detailed in the section "Constants and Pointers" on page 27.

An attempt to pass the address of an integer literal as shown below will also generate a syntax error:

```
passingAddressOfConstants(&23, &23);
```

In this case, the error message will indicate that an lvalue is required as the address-of operator's operand. The concept of an lvalue is discussed in "Dereferencing a Pointer Using the Indirection Operator" on page 11.

Returning a Pointer

Returning a pointer is easy to do. We simply declare the return type to be a pointer to the appropriate data type. If we need to return an object from a function, the following two techniques are frequently used:

- Allocate memory within the function using malloc and return its address. The caller is responsible for deallocating the memory returned.

- Pass an object to the function where it is modified. This makes the allocation and deallocation of the object's memory the caller's responsibility.

First, we will illustrate the use of malloc type functions to allocate the memory returned. This is followed by an example where we return a pointer to a local object. This latter approach is not recommended. The approach identified in the second bullet is then illustrated in the section "Passing Null Pointers" on page 67.

In the following example, we define a function that is passed the size of an integer array and a value to initialize each element. The function allocates memory for an integer array, initializes the array to the value passed, and then returns the array's address:

```
int* allocateArray(int size, int value) {
    int* arr = (int*)malloc(size * sizeof(int));
    for(int i=0; i<size; i++) {
        arr[i] = value;
    }
    return arr;
}
```

The following illustrates how this function can be used:

```
int* vector = allocateArray(5,45);
for(int i=0; i<5; i++) {
    printf("%d\n", vector[i]);
}
```

Figure 3-5 illustrates how memory is allocated for this function. The Before image shows the program's state right before the return statement is executed. The After image shows the program's state after the function has returned. The variable vector now contains the address of the memory allocated in the function. While the arr variable went away when the function terminated, the memory referenced by the pointer does not go away. This memory will eventually need to be freed.

Although the previous example works correctly, several potential problems can occur when returning a pointer from a function, including:

- Returning an uninitialized pointer
- Returning a pointer to an invalid address
- Returning a pointer to a local variable
- Returning a pointer but failing to free it

The last problem is typified by the allocateArray function. Returning dynamically allocated memory from the function means the function's caller is responsible for deallocating it. Consider the following example:

```
int* vector = allocateArray(5,45);
...
free(vector);
```

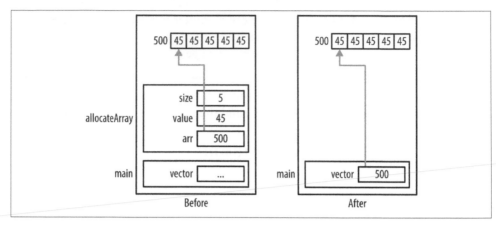

Figure 3-5. Returning a pointer

We must eventually free it once we are through using it. If we don't, then we will have a memory leak.

Pointers to Local Data

Returning a pointer to local data is an easy mistake to make if you don't understand how the program stack works. In the following example, we rework the `allocateAr ray` function used in the section "Returning a Pointer" on page 64. Instead of dynamically allocating memory for the array, we used a local array:

```
int* allocateArray(int size, int value) {
    int arr[size];
    for(int i=0; i<size; i++) {
        arr[i] = value;
    }
    return arr;
}
```

Unfortunately, the address of the array returned is no longer valid once the function returns because the function's stack frame is popped off the stack. While each array element may still contain a 45, these values may be overwritten if another function is called. This is illustrated with the following sequence. Here, the `printf` function is invoked repeatedly, resulting in corruption of the array:

```
int* vector = allocateArray(5,45);
for(int i=0; i<5; i++) {
    printf("%d\n", vector[i]);
}
```

Figure 3-6 illustrates how memory is allocated when this happens. The dashed box shows where other stack frames, such as those used by the printf function, may be pushed onto the program stack, thus corrupting the memory held by the array. The actual contents of that stack frame are implementation-dependent.

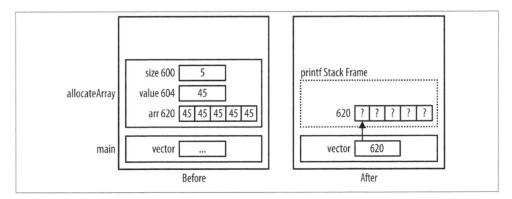

Figure 3-6. Returning a pointer to local data

An alternative approach is to declare the arr variable as static. This will restrict the variable's scope to the function but allocate it outside of the stack frame, eliminating the possibility of another function overwriting the variable's value:

```
int* allocateArray(int size, int value) {
    static int arr[5];
    ...
}
```

However, this will not always work. Every time the allocateArray function is called, it will reuse the array. This effectively invalidates any previous calls to the function. In addition, the static array must be declared with a fixed size. This will limit the function's ability to handle various array sizes.

If the function returns only a few possible values and it does not hurt to share them, then it can maintain a list of these values and return the appropriate one. This can be useful if we are returning a status type message, such as an error number that is not likely to be modified. In the section "Returning Strings" on page 126, an example of using global and static values is demonstrated.

Passing Null Pointers

In the following version of the allocateArray function, a pointer to an array is passed along with its size and a value that it will use to initialize each element of the array. The pointer is returned for convenience. Although this version of the function does not allocate memory, later versions will allocate memory:

```
int* allocateArray(int *arr, int size, int value) {
    if(arr != NULL) {
        for(int i=0; i<size; i++) {
            arr[i] = value;
        }
    }
    return arr;
}
```

When a pointer is passed to a function, it is always good practice to verify it is not null before using it.

The function can be invoked as follows:

```
int* vector = (int*)malloc(5 * sizeof(int));
allocateArray(vector,5,45);
```

If the pointer is NULL, then no action is performed and the program will execute without terminating abnormally.

Passing a Pointer to a Pointer

When a pointer is passed to a function, it is passed by value. If we want to modify the original pointer and not the copy of the pointer, we need to pass it as a pointer to a pointer. In the following example, a pointer to an integer array is passed, which will be assigned memory and initialized. The function will return the allocated memory back through the first parameter. In the function, we first allocate memory and then initialize it. The address of this allocated memory is intended to be assigned to a pointer to an int. To modify this pointer in the calling function, we need to pass the pointer's address. Thus, the parameter is declared as a pointer to a pointer to an int. In the calling function, we need to pass the address of the pointer:

```
void allocateArray(int **arr, int size, int value) {
    *arr = (int*)malloc(size * sizeof(int));
    if(*arr != NULL) {
        for(int i=0; i<size; i++) {
            *(*arr+i) = value;
        }
    }
}
```

The function can be tested using the following code:

```
int *vector = NULL;
allocateArray(&vector,5,45);
```

The first parameter to allocateArray is passed as a pointer to a pointer to an integer. When we call the function, we need to pass a value of this type. This is done by passing the address of vector. The address returned by malloc is assigned to arr. Dereferencing a pointer to a pointer to an integer results in a pointer to an integer. Because this is the address of vector, we modify vector.

The memory allocation is illustrated in Figure 3-7. The Before image shows the stack's state after malloc returns and the array is initialized. Likewise, the After image shows the stack's state after the function returns.

To easily identify problems such as memory leaks, draw a diagram of memory allocation.

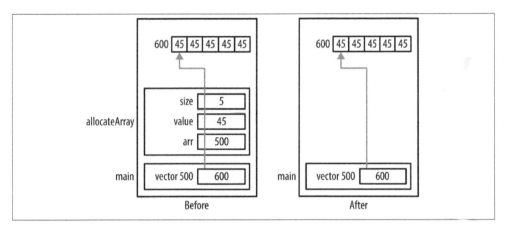

Figure 3-7. Passing a pointer to a pointer

The following version of the function illustrates why passing a simple pointer will not work:

```
void allocateArray(int *arr, int size, int value) {
    arr = (int*)malloc(size * sizeof(int));
    if(arr != NULL) {
        for(int i=0; i<size; i++) {
            arr[i] = value;
        }
    }
}
```

The following sequence illustrates using the function:

```
int *vector = NULL;
allocateArray(&vector,5,45);
printf("%p\n",vector);
```

When the program is executed you will see 0x0 displayed because when vector is passed to the function, its value is copied into the parameter arr. Modifying arr has no effect on vector. When the function returns, the value stored in arr is not copied to vector. Figure 3-8 illustrates the allocation of memory. The Before malloc image shows the state of memory just before arr is assigned a new value. It contains the value of NULL, which was passed to it from vector. The After malloc image shows the state of memory after the malloc function was executed in the allocateArray function and the array was initialized. The variable arr has been modified to point to a new place in the heap. The After return image shows the program stack's state after the function returns. In addition, we have a memory leak because we have lost access to the block of memory at address 600.

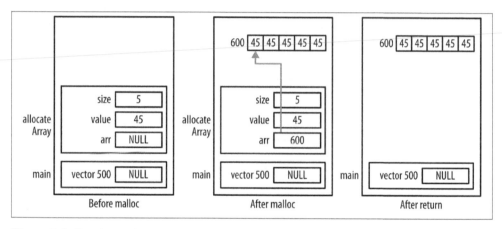

Figure 3-8. Passing pointers

Writing your own free function

Several issues surround the free function that encourage some programmers to create their own version of this function. The free function does not check the pointer passed to see whether it is NULL and does not set the pointer to NULL before it returns. Setting a pointer to NULL after freeing is a good practice.

Given the foundation provided in the section "Passing and Returning by Pointer" on page 61, the following illustrates one way of implementing your own free function that assigns a NULL value to the pointer. It requires that we use a pointer to a pointer:

```
void saferFree(void **pp) {
    if (pp != NULL && *pp != NULL) {
        free(*pp);
        *pp = NULL;
    }
}
```

The `saferFree` function calls the `free` function that actually deallocates the memory. Its parameter is declared as a pointer to a pointer to `void`. Using a pointer to a pointer allows us to modify the pointer passed. Using the `void` type allows all types of pointers to be passed. However, we get a warning if we do not explicitly cast the pointer type to void when we call the function. If we explicitly perform the cast, then the warning goes away.

The `safeFree` macro, shown below, calls the `saferFree` function with this cast and uses the address-of operator, thus alleviating the need for a function's user to perform the cast and to pass the pointer's address.

```
#define safeFree(p) saferFree((void**)&(p))
```

The next sequence illustrates the use of this macro:

```
int main() {
    int *pi;
    pi = (int*) malloc(sizeof(int));
    *pi = 5;
    printf("Before: %p\n",pi);
    safeFree(pi);
    printf("After: %p\n",pi);
    safeFree(pi);
    return (EXIT_SUCCESS);
}
```

Assuming `malloc` returned memory from address 1000, the output of this sequence will be 1000 and then 0. The second use of the `safeFree` macro with a `NULL` value does not terminate the application, as the function detects and ignores it.

Function Pointers

A function pointer is a pointer that holds the address of a function. The ability of pointers to point to functions turns out to be an important and useful feature of C. This provides us with another way of executing functions in an order that may not be known at compile time and without using conditional statements.

One concern regarding the use of function pointers is a potentially slower running program. The processor may not be able to use branch prediction in conjunction with pipelining. Branch prediction is a technique whereby the processor will guess which multiple execution sequences will be executed. Pipelining is a hardware technology commonly used to improve processor performance and is achieved by overlapping instruction execution. In this scheme, the processor will start processing the branch it believes will be executed. If the processor successfully predicts the correct branch, then the instructions currently in the pipeline will not have to be discarded.

This slowdown may or may not be realized. The use of function pointers in situations such as table lookups can mitigate performance issues. In this section, we will learn how to declare function pointers, see how they can be used to support alternate execution paths, and explore techniques that exploit their potential.

Declaring Function Pointers

The syntax for declaring a pointer to a function can be confusing when you first see it. As with many aspects of C, once you get used to the notation, things start falling into place. Let's start with a simple declaration. Below, we declare a pointer to a function that is passed void and returns void:

```
void (*foo)();
```

This declaration looks a lot like a function prototype. If we removed the first set of parentheses, it would appear to be a function prototype for the function foo, which is passed void and returns a pointer to void. However, the parentheses make it a function pointer with a name of foo. The asterisk indicates that it is a pointer. Figure 3-9 highlights the parts of a function pointer declaration.

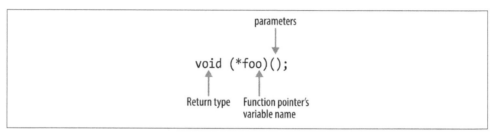

Figure 3-9. Function pointer declaration

 When function pointers are used, the programmer must be careful to ensure it is used properly because C does not check to see whether the correct parameters are passed.

Other examples of function pointer declarations are illustrated below:

```
int (*f1)(double);      // Passed a double and
                        //    returns an int
void (*f2)(char*);      // Passed a pointer to char and
                        //    returns void
double* (*f3)(int, int); // Passed two integers and
                        //    returns a pointer to a double
```

 One suggested naming convention for function pointers is to always begin their name with the prefix: fptr.

Do not confuse functions that return a pointer with function pointers. The following declares f4 as a function that returns a pointer to an integer, while f5 is a function pointer that returns an integer. The variable f6 is a function pointer that returns a pointer to an integer:

```
int  *f4();
int  (*f5)();
int* (*f6)();
```

The whitespace within these expressions can be rearranged so that it reads as follows:

```
int*  f4();
int (*f5)();
```

It is clear that f4 is a function that returns a pointer to an integer. However, using parentheses with f5 clearly bind the "pointer" asterisk to the function name, making it a function pointer.

Using a Function Pointer

Below is a simple example using a function pointer where a function is passed an integer and returns an integer. We also define a square function that squares an integer and then returns the square. To simplify these examples, we ignore the possibility of integer overflow.

```
int (*fptr1)(int);

int square(int num) {
    return num*num;
}
```

To use the function pointer to execute the square function, we need to assign the square function's address to the function pointer, as shown below. As with array names, when we use the name of a function by itself, it returns the function's address. We also declare an integer that we will pass to the function:

```
int n = 5;
fptr1 = square;
printf("%d squared is %d\n",n, fptr1(n));
```

When executed it will display: "5 squared is 25." We could have used the address-of operator with the function name as follows, but it is not necessary and is redundant. The compiler will effectively ignore the address-of operator when used in this context.

```
fptr1 = &square;
```

Figure 3-10 illustrates how memory is allocated for this example. We have placed the square function below the program stack. This is for illustrative purposes only. Functions are allocated in a different segment than that used by the program stack. The function's actual location is normally not of interest.

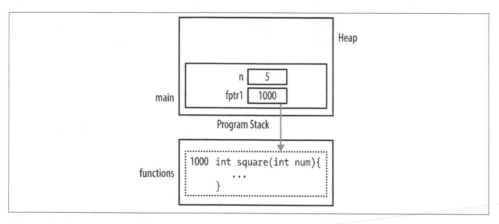

Figure 3-10. *Location of functions*

It is convenient to declare a type definition for function pointers. This is illustrated below for the previous function pointer. The type definition looks a little bit strange. Normally, the type definition's name is the declaration's last element:

```
typedef int (*funcptr)(int);

...

funcptr fptr2;
fptr2 = square;
printf("%d squared is %d\n",n, fptr2(n));
```

"Function Pointers and Strings" on page 130 provides an interesting example with respect to using a function pointer to control how an array of strings is sorted.

Passing Function Pointers

Passing a function pointer is easy enough to do. Simply use a function pointer declaration as a parameter of a function. We will demonstrate passing a function pointer using add, sub, and compute functions as declared below:

```
int add(int num1, int num2) {
    return num1 + num2;
}

int sub(int num1, int num2) {
    return num1 - num2;
}

typedef int (*fptrOperation)(int,int);

int compute(fptrOperation operation, int num1, int num2) {
```

```
        return operation(num1, num2);
    }
```

The following sequence demonstrates these functions:

```
        printf("%d\n",compute(add,5,6));
        printf("%d\n",compute(sub,5,6));
```

The output will be an 11 and a −1. The add and sub function's addresses were passed to the compute function. These addresses were then used to invoke the corresponding operation. This example also shows how code can be made more flexible through the use of function pointers.

Returning Function Pointers

Returning a function pointer requires declaring the function's return type as a function pointer. To demonstrate how this is done, we will reuse the add and sub function along with the type definition we developed in the section "Passing Function Pointers" on page 74.

We will use the following select function to return a function pointer to an operation based in a character input. It will return a pointer to either the add function or the subtract function, depending on the opcode passed:

```
    fptrOperation select(char opcode) {
        switch(opcode) {
            case '+': return add;
            case '-': return subtract;
        }
    }
```

The evaluate function ties these functions together. The function is passed two integers and a character representing the operation to be performed. It passes the opcode to the select function, which returns a pointer to the function to execute. In the return statement, it executes this function and returns the result:

```
    int evaluate(char opcode, int num1, int num2) {
        fptrOperation operation = select(opcode);
        return operation(num1, num2);
    }
```

This function is demonstrated with the following printf statements:

```
        printf("%d\n",evaluate('+', 5, 6));
        printf("%d\n",evaluate('-', 5, 6));
```

The output will be an 11 and a −1.

Using an Array of Function Pointers

Arrays of function pointers can be used to select the function to evaluate on the basis of some criteria. Declaring such an array is straightforward. We simply use the function pointer declaration as the array's type, as shown below. The array is also initialized to all NULLs. When a block of initialization values are used with an array, its values will be assigned to consecutive elements of the array. If the number of values is less than the size of the array, as in this example, then the remaining elements of the array are initialized to 0:

```
typedef int (*operation)(int, int);
operation operations[128] = {NULL};
```

Alternatively, we can declare this array without using a typedef as shown below:

```
int (*operations[128])(int, int) = {NULL};
```

The intent of this array is to allow a character index to select a corresponding function to execute. For example, the '*' character will identify the multiplication function if it exists. We can use character indexes because a character literal is an integer. The 128 elements corresponds to the first 128 ASCII characters. We will use this definition in conjunction with the add and subtract functions developed in the section "Returning Function Pointers" on page 75.

Having initialized the array to all NULLs, we then assign the add and subtract functions to the elements corresponding to the plus and minus signs:

```
void initializeOperationsArray() {
    operations['+'] = add;
    operations['-'] = subtract;
}
```

The previous evaluate function is rewritten as evaluateArray. Instead of calling the select function to obtain a function pointer, we used the operations with the operation character as an index:

```
int evaluateArray(char opcode, int num1, int num2) {
    fptrOperation operation;
    operation = operations[opcode];
    return operation(num1, num2);
}
```

Test the functions using the following sequence:

```
initializeOperationsArray();
printf("%d\n",evaluateArray('+', 5, 6));
printf("%d\n",evaluateArray('-', 5, 6));
```

The results of executing this sequence are 11 and –1. A more robust version of the evaluateArray function would check for null function pointers before trying to execute the function.

Comparing Function Pointers

Function pointers can be compared to one another using the equality and inequality operators. In the following example, we use the fptrOperator type definition and the add function from the section "Passing Function Pointers" on page 74. The add function is assigned to the fptr1 function pointer and then compared against the add function's address:

```
fptrOperation fptr1 = add;

if(fptr1 == add) {
    printf("fptr1 points to add function\n");
} else {
    printf("fptr1 does not point to add function\n");
}
```

When this is executed, the output will verify that the pointer does point to the add function.

A more realistic example of where the comparison of function pointers would be useful involves an array of function pointers that represent the steps of a task. For example, we may have a series of functions that manipulate an array of inventory parts. One set of operations may be to sort the parts, calculate a cumulative sum of their quantities, and then display the array and sum. A second set of operations may be to display the array, find the most expensive and the least expensive, and then display their difference. Each operation could be defined by an array of pointers to the individual functions. A log operation may be present in both lists. The ability to compare two function pointers would permit the dynamic modification of an operation by deleting the operation, such as logging, by finding and then removing the function from the list.

Casting Function Pointers

A pointer to one function can be cast to another type. This should be done with care since the runtime system does not verify that parameters used by a function pointer are correct. It is also possible to cast a function pointer to a different function pointer and then back. The resulting pointer will be equal to the original pointer. The size of function pointers used are not necessarily the same. The following sequence illustrates this operation:

```
typedef int (*fptrToSingleInt)(int);
typedef int (*fptrToTwoInts)(int,int);
int add(int, int);

fptrToTwoInts fptrFirst = add;
fptrToSingleInt fptrSecond = (fptrToSingleInt)fptrFirst;
fptrFirst = (fptrToTwoInts)fptrSecond;
printf("%d\n",fptrFirst(5,6));
```

This sequence, when executed, will display 11 as its output.

 Conversion between function pointers and pointers to data is not guaranteed to work.

The use of `void*` is not guaranteed to work with function pointers. That is, we should not assign a function pointer to `void*` as shown below:

```
void* pv = add;
```

However, when interchanging function pointers, it is common to see a "base" function pointer type as declared below. This declares `fptrBase` as a function pointer to a function, which is passed void and returns void:

```
typedef void (*fptrBase)();
```

The following sequence demonstrate the use of this base pointer, which duplicates the previous example:

```
fptrBase basePointer;
fptrFirst = add;
basePointer = (fptrToSingleInt)fptrFirst;
fptrFirst = (fptrToTwoInts)basePointer;
printf("%d\n",fptrFirst(5,6));
```

A base pointer is used as a placeholder to exchange function pointer values.

 Always make sure you use the correct argument list for function pointers. Failure to do so will result in indeterminate behavior.

Summary

Understanding the program stack and heap structures contributes to a more detailed and thorough understanding of how a program works and how pointers behave. In this chapter, we examined the stack, the heap, and the stack frame. These concepts help explain the mechanics of passing and returning pointers to and from a function.

For example, returning a pointer to a local variable is bad because the memory allocated to the local variable will be overwritten by subsequent function calls. Passing a pointer to constant data is efficient and prevents the function from modifying the data passed. Passing a pointer to a pointer allows the argument pointer to be reassigned to a different location in memory. The stack and heap helped detail and illustrate this functionality.

Function pointers were also introduced and explained. This type of pointer is useful for controlling the execution sequence within an application by allowing alternate functions to be executed based on the application's needs.

CHAPTER 4
Pointers and Arrays

An array is a fundamental data structure built into C. A thorough understanding of arrays and their use is necessary to develop effective applications. Misunderstandings of array and pointer usage can result in hard-to-find errors and less than optimal performance in applications. Array and pointer notations are closely related to each other and can frequently be used interchangeably in the right context.

A common misconception is that an array and a pointer are completely interchangeable. An array name is not a pointer. Although an array name can be treated as a pointer at times, and array notation can be used with pointers, they are distinct and cannot always be used in place of each other. Understanding this difference will help you avoid incorrect use of these notations. For example, although the name of an array used by itself will return the array's address, we cannot use the name by itself as the target of an assignment.

Arrays support many parts of an application and can be single or multidimensional. In this chapter, we will address the fundamental aspects of arrays as they relate to pointers to provide you with a deep understanding of arrays and the various ways they can be manipulated with pointers. You will see their use in more advanced contexts throughout the book.

We start with a quick review of arrays and then examine the similarities and differences between array and pointer notation. Arrays can be created using `malloc` type functions. These functions provide more flexibility than that afforded by traditional array declarations. We will see how the `realloc` function can be used to change the amount of memory allocated for an array.

Dynamically allocating memory for an array can present challenges, especially when we are dealing with arrays with two or more dimensions, as we have to ensure that the array is allocated in contiguous memory.

We will also explore problems that can occur when passing and returning arrays. In most situations, the array's size must be passed so the array can be properly handled in a function. There is nothing inherent in an array's internal representation that determines its length. If we do not pass the length, the function has no standard means of knowing where the array ends. We will also examine how to create jagged arrays in C, although they are infrequently used. A jagged array is a two-dimensional array where each row may have a different number of columns.

To demonstrate these concepts, we will use a vector for single-dimensional arrays and a matrix for two-dimensional arrays. Vectors and matrices have found extensive use in many areas, including analyzing electromagnetic fields, weather prediction, and in mathematics.

Quick Review of Arrays

An array is a contiguous collection of homogeneous elements that can be accessed using an index. By contiguous, we mean the elements of the array are adjacent to one another in memory with no gaps between them. By homogeneous, we mean they are all of the same type. Array declarations use a set of brackets and can possess multiple dimensions.

Two-dimensional arrays are common, and we typically use the terms *rows* and *columns* to describe the position of an array's element. Arrays with three or more dimensions are not as common but can be quite useful in some applications. A two-dimensional array is not to be confused with an array of pointers. They are similar but behave slightly differently, as will be shown in the section "Using a One-Dimensional Array of Pointers" on page 92.

Variable length arrays were introduced in C99 version of C. Previously, techniques using the realloc function were used to support arrays whose sizes change. We illustrate the realloc function in the section "Using the realloc Function to Resize an Array" on page 87.

 Arrays have a fixed size. When we declare an array, we need to decide how big it should be. If we specify too many elements, we waste space. If we specify too few elements, we limit how many elements we can process. The realloc function and variable length arrays provide techniques for dealing with arrays whose size needs to change. With a little work, we can resize an array and use just the right amount of memory.

One-Dimensional Arrays

A one-dimensional array is a linear structure. It uses a single index to access its members. The following is a declaration of a five-element array of integers:

```
int vector[5];
```

Array indexes start with 0 and end at one less than their declared size. Valid indexes for the array vector start at 0 and end at 4. However, C does not enforce these bounds. Using an invalid index for an array can result in unpredictable behavior. Figure 4-1 illustrates how the array is allocated in memory. Each element is four bytes in length and is uninitialized. Depending on the memory model used, as explained in "Memory Models" on page 16, the size may be different.

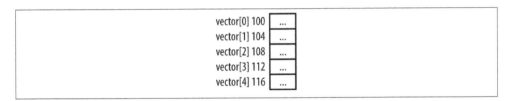

Figure 4-1. Array memory allocation

The internal representation of an array has no information about the number of elements it contains. The array name simply references a block of memory. Using the sizeof operator with an array will return the number of bytes allocated to the array. To determine the number of elements, we divide the array's size by its element's size, as illustrated below. This will display 5:

```
printf("%d\n", sizeof(vector)/sizeof(int));
```

One-dimensional arrays can be readily initialized using a block type statement. In the following sequence, each element is initialized to an integer starting at one:

```
int vector[5] = {1, 2, 3, 4, 5};
```

Two-Dimensional Arrays

Two-dimensional arrays use rows and columns to identify array elements. This type of array needs to be mapped to the one-dimension address space of main memory. In C this is achieved by using a row-column ordering sequence. The array's first row is placed in memory followed by the second row, then the third row, and this ordering continues until the last row is placed in memory.

The following declares a two-dimensional array with two rows and three columns. The array is initialized using a block statement. Figure 4-2 illustrates how memory is allocated for this array. The diagram on the left shows how memory is mapped. The diagram on the right shows how it can be viewed conceptually:

```
int matrix[2][3] = {{1,2,3},{4,5,6}};
```

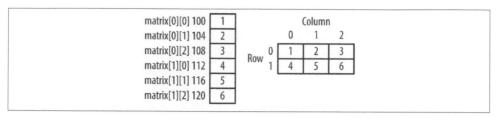

Figure 4-2. Two-dimensional array

A two-dimensional array is treated as an array of arrays. That is, when we access the array using only one subscript, we get a pointer to the corresponding row. This is demonstrated in the following code sequence where each row's address and size is displayed:

```
for (int i = 0; i < 2; i++) {
    printf("&matrix[%d]: %p  sizeof(matrix[%d]): %d\n",
            i, &matrix[i], i, sizeof(matrix[i]));
}
```

The following output assumes the array is located at address 100. The size is 12 because each row has three elements of four bytes each:

```
&matrix[0]: 100 sizeof(matrix[0]): 12
&matrix[1]: 112 sizeof(matrix[1]): 12
```

In the section "Pointers and Multidimensional Arrays" on page 94, we will examine this behavior in more detail.

Multidimensional Arrays

Multidimensional arrays have two or more dimensions. As with two-dimensional arrays, multiple sets of brackets define the array's type and size. In the following example, we define a three-dimensional array consisting of three rows, two columns, and a rank of four. The term *rank* is often used to denote the elements of the third dimension:

```
int arr3d[3][2][4] = {
    {{1, 2, 3, 4}, {5, 6, 7, 8}},
    {{9, 10, 11, 12}, {13, 14, 15, 16}},
    {{17, 18, 19, 20}, {21, 22, 23, 24}}
};
```

The elements are allocated contiguously in row-column-rank order as illustrated in Figure 4-3.

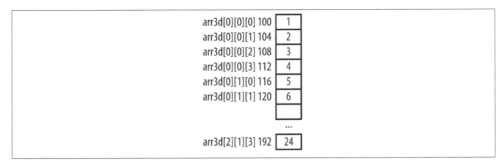

Figure 4-3. Three-dimensional array

We will use these declarations in later examples.

Pointer Notation and Arrays

Pointers can be very useful when working with arrays. We can use them with existing arrays or to allocate memory from the heap and then treat the memory as if it were an array. Array notation and pointer notation can be used somewhat interchangeably. However, they are not exactly the same as detailed in the section "Differences Between Arrays and Pointers" on page 85.

When an array name is used by itself, the array's address is returned. We can assign this address to a pointer as illustrated below:

```
int vector[5] = {1, 2, 3, 4, 5};
int *pv = vector;
```

The variable pv is a pointer to the first element of the array and not the array itself. When we first assigned a value to pv, we assigned the address of the array's first element.

We can use either the array name by itself or use the address-of operator with the array's first element as illustrated below. These are equivalent and will return the address of vector. Using the address-of operator is more verbose but also more explicit:

```
printf("%p\n",vector);
printf("%p\n",&vector[0]);
```

The expression &vector is sometimes used to obtain the address of an array. It differs from the other notations in that it returns a pointer to the entire array. The other two approaches yield a pointer to an integer. Instead of returning a pointer to an integer, it returns a pointer to an array of integers. The use of this type will be illustrated in the section "Passing a Multidimensional Array" on page 96.

We can also use array subscripts with pointers. Effectively, the notation pv[i] is evaluated as:

```
*(pv + i)
```

The pointer pv contains the address of a block of memory. The bracket notation will take the address contained in pv and adds the value contained in the index i using pointer arithmetic. This new address is then dereferenced to return its contents.

As we discussed in the section "Pointer Arithmetic" on page 20, adding an integer to a pointer will increment the address it holds by the product of the integer and the data type's size. The same is true if we add an integer to the name of an array. The following two statements are equivalent:

```
*(pv + i)
*(vector + i)
```

Assume the vector is located at address 100 and pv is located at address 96. Table 4-1 and Figure 4-4 illustrate the use of array subscripts and pointer arithmetic with both the array name and the pointer for various values.

Table 4-1. Array/pointer notation

Value	Equivalent Expression			
92	&vector[-2]	vector - 2	&pv[-2]	pv - 2
100	vector	vector+0	&pv[0]	pv
100	&vector[0]	vector+0	&pv[0]	pv
104	&vector[1]	vector + 1	&pv[1]	pv + 1
140	&vector[10]	vector + 10	&pv[10]	pv + 10

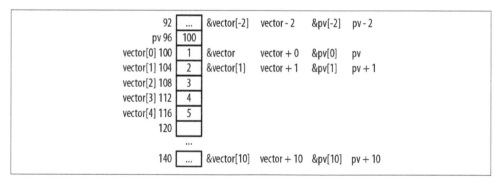

Figure 4-4. Array/pointer notation

When we add 1 to the array address we effectively add 4, the size of an integer, to the address since this is an array of integers. With the first and last operations, we addressed locations outside the array's bounds. While this is not a good practice, it does emphasize the need to be careful when using indexes or pointers to access elements of an array.

Array notation can be thought of as a "shift and dereference" operation. The expression vector[2] means start with vector, which is a pointer to the beginning of the array, shift two positions to the right, and then dereference that location to fetch its value. Using the address-of operator in conjunction with array notation, as in &vector[2], essentially cancels out the dereferencing. It can be interpreted as go left two positions and then return that address.

The following demonstrates the use of pointers in the implementation of the scalar addition operation. This operation takes a value and multiplies it against each element of the vector:

```
pv = vector;
int value = 3;
for(int i=0; i<5; i++) {
    *pv++ *= value;
}
```

Differences Between Arrays and Pointers

There are several differences between the use of arrays and the use of pointers to arrays. In this section, we will use the vector array and pv pointer as defined below:

```
int vector[5] = {1, 2, 3, 4, 5};
int *pv = vector;
```

The code generated by vector[i] is different from the code generated by *(vector +i). The notation vector[i] generates machine code that starts at location vector, *moves* i positions from this location, and uses its content. The notation *(vector+i) generates machine code that starts at location vector, *adds* i to the address, and then uses the contents at that address. While the result is the same, the generated machine code is different. This difference is rarely of significance to most programmers.

There is a difference when the sizeof operator is applied to an array and to a pointer to the same array. Applying the sizeof operator to vector will return 20, the number of bytes allocated to the array. Applying the sizeof operator against pv will return 4, the pointer's size.

The pointer pv is an lvalue. An lvalue denotes the term used on the lefthand side of an assignment operator. An lvalue must be capable of being modified. An array name such as vector is not an lvalue and cannot be modified. The address assigned to an array cannot be changed. A pointer can be assigned a new value and reference a different section of memory.

Consider the following:

```
pv = pv + 1;
vector = vector + 1; // Syntax error
```

We cannot modify vector, only its contents. However, the expression vector+1 is fine, as demonstrated below:

```
pv = vector + 1;
```

Using malloc to Create a One-Dimensional Array

If we allocate memory from the heap and assign the address to a pointer, there is no reason we cannot use array subscripts with the pointer and treat this memory as an array. In the following sequence, we duplicate the contents of the vector array used earlier:

```
int *pv = (int*) malloc(5 * sizeof(int));
for(int i=0; i<5; i++) {
    pv[i] = i+1;
}
```

We could have used pointer notation as shown below; however, the array notation is often easier to follow:

```
for(int i=0; i<5; i++) {
    *(pv+i) = i+1;
}
```

Figure 4-5 illustrates how memory is allocated for this example.

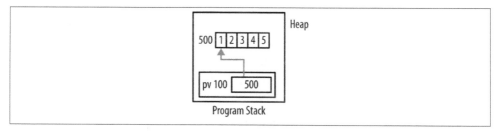

Figure 4-5. Array allocated from the heap

This technique creates a region of memory and treats it as an array. Its size is determined at runtime. However, we need to remember to deallocate the memory when we are through with it.

 In the previous example we used *(pv+i) instead of *pv+i. Since the dereference operator has higher precedence than the plus operator, the second expression's pointer is dereferenced, giving us the value referenced by the pointer. We then add i to this integer value. This was not what was intended. In addition, when we use this expression as an lvalue, the compiler will complain. Thus, we need to force the addition to be performed first, followed by the dereference operation, in order for it to work correctly.

Using the realloc Function to Resize an Array

We can resize an existing array created using `malloc` with the `realloc` function. The essentials of the `realloc` function were detailed in Chapter 2. The C standard C99 supports variable length arrays. In some situations, this may prove to be a better solution than using the `realloc` function. If you are not using C99, then the `realloc` function will need to be used. Also, variable length arrays can only be declared as a member of a function. If the array is needed longer than the function's duration, then `realloc` will need to be used.

To illustrate the `realloc` function, we will implement a function to read in characters from standard input and assign them to a buffer. The buffer will contain all of the characters read in except for a terminating return character. Since we do not know how many characters the user will input, we do not know how long the buffer should be. We will use the `realloc` function to allocate additional space by a fixed increment amount. The code to implement this function is shown below:

```c
char* getLine(void) {
    const size_t sizeIncrement = 10;
    char* buffer = malloc(sizeIncrement);
    char* currentPosition = buffer;
    size_t maximumLength = sizeIncrement;
    size_t length = 0;
    int character;

    if(currentPosition == NULL) { return NULL; }

    while(1) {
        character = fgetc(stdin);
        if(character == '\n') { break; }

        if(++length >= maximumLength) {
            char *newBuffer = realloc(buffer, maximumLength += sizeIncrement);

            if(newBuffer == NULL) {
                free(buffer);
                return NULL;
            }

            currentPosition = newBuffer + (currentPosition - buffer);
            buffer = newBuffer;
        }
        *currentPosition++ = character;
    }
    *currentPosition = '\0';
    return buffer;
}
```

We will start by defining a series of declarations as summarized in Table 4-2.

Table 4-2. getLine variables

sizeIncrement	The size of the initial buffer and the amount it will be incremented by when the buffer needs to be enlarged
buffer	A pointer to the characters read in
currentPosition	A pointer to the next free position in the buffer
maximumLength	The maximum number of characters that can be safely stored in the buffer
length	The number of characters read in
character	The last character read in

The buffer is created with a size of `sizeIncrement`. If the `malloc` function is unable to allocate memory, the first `if` statement will force the function to return NULL. An infinite loop is entered where the characters are processed one at a time. When the loop exits, a NUL is added to terminate the string and the buffer's address is returned.

Within the `while` loop, a character is read in. If it is a carriage return, the loop is exited. Next, the `if` statement determines whether we have exceeded the buffer's size. Otherwise, the character is added to the current position within the buffer.

If we have exceeded the buffer's size, the `realloc` function creates a new block of memory. This block is `sizeIncrement` bytes larger than the old one. If it is unable to allocate memory, we free up the existing allocated memory and force the function to return NULL. Otherwise, `currentPosition` is adjusted to point to the right position within the new buffer and we assign the variable buffer to point to the newly allocated buffer. The `realloc` function will not necessarily keep your existing memory in place, so you have to use the pointer it returns to figure out where your new, resized memory block is.

The variable `newBuffer` holds the allocated memory's address. We needed a separate variable, not `buffer`, in case the `realloc` was unable to allocate memory. This allows us to detect and handle the condition.

We did not free `buffer` if `realloc` was successful because `realloc` will copy the original buffer to the new buffer and free up the old buffer. If we had tried to free `buffer`, then it would normally result in the program's termination because we tried to free the same block of memory twice.

Figure 4-6 illustrates memory being allocated for the `getLine` function with an input string of "Once upon a time there was a giant pumpkin." The program stack has been simplified to ignore the local variables except for `buffer` and `currentPosition`. The buffer has been extended four times, as indicated by the rectangle containing the input string.

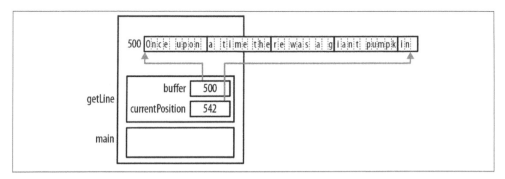

Figure 4-6. Memory allocation for getLine function

The realloc function can also be used to decrease the amount of space used by a pointer. To illustrate its use, the trim function shown below will remove leading blanks in a string:

```c
char* trim(char* phrase) {
    char* old = phrase;
    char* new = phrase;

    while(*old == ' ') {
        old++;
    }

    while(*old) {
        *(new++) = *(old++);
    }
    *new = 0;
    return (char*) realloc(phrase,strlen(phrase)+1);
}

int main() {
    char* buffer = (char*)malloc(strlen("  cat")+1);
    strcpy(buffer,"  cat");
    printf("%s\n",trim(buffer));
}
```

The first while loop uses the old variable to skip over any leading blanks. The second while loop copies the remaining characters in the string to the beginning of the string. It will evaluate to true until NUL is reached, which will evaluate to false. A zero is then added to terminate the string. The realloc function is then used to reallocate the memory based on the string's new length.

Figure 4-7 illustrates the function's use with an original string of " cat". The state of string before and after the trim function executes is shown. The shaded memory is the old memory and should not be accessed.

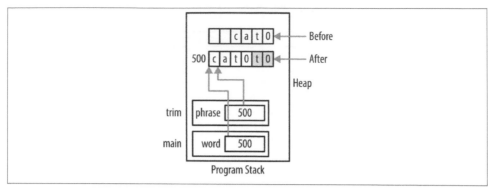

Figure 4-7. Realloc example

Passing a One-Dimensional Array

When a one-dimensional array is passed to a function, the array's address is passed by value. This makes the transfer of information more efficient since we are not passing the entire array and having to allocate memory in the stack for it. Normally, this means the array's size must be passed. If we don't, from the function's perspective all we have is the address of an array with no indication of its size.

Unless there is something integral to the array to tell us its bounds, we need to pass the size information when we pass the array. In the case of a string stored in an array, we can rely on the NUL termination character to tell us when we can stop processing the array. We will examine this in Chapter 5. Generally, if we do not know the array's size, we are unable to process its elements and can wind up working with too few elements or treating memory outside of the array as if it were part of the array. This will frequently result in abnormal program termination.

We can declare the array in the function declaration using one of two notations: array notation or pointer notation.

Using Array Notation

In the following example, an integer array is passed to a function along with its size. Its contents are then displayed:

```
void displayArray(int arr[], int size) {
    for (int i = 0; i < size; i++) {
        printf("%d\n", arr[i]);
    }
}

    int vector[5] = {1, 2, 3, 4, 5};
    displayArray(vector, 5);
```

The sequence's output will be the numbers 1 through 5. We passed the number 5 to the function that indicates its size. We could have passed any positive number and the function would attempt to display the corresponding number of elements, regardless of whether the size was correct. The program may terminate if we attempt to address memory outside of the array's bounds. The memory allocation for this example is shown in Figure 4-8.

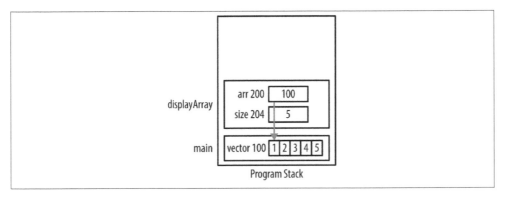

Figure 4-8. Using array notation

 A common mistake is to use the `sizeof` operator with the array in order to determine its number of elements, as shown below. However, as explained in the section "One-Dimensional Arrays" on page 80, this is not the correct way of determining its size. In this case, we would be passing the value of 20 to the array.

```
displayArray(arr, sizeof(arr));
```

It is a common practice to pass a size smaller than the actual number of elements in an array. This is done to process only part of an array. For example, assume we read in a series of ages into an array but did not fill up the array. If we called a `sort` function to sort it, we would only want to sort the valid ages, not every array element.

Using Pointer Notation

We do not have to use the bracket notation when declaring an array parameter of a function. Instead, we can use pointer notation as follows:

```
void displayArray(int* arr, int size) {
    for (int i = 0; i < size; i++) {
        printf("%d\n", arr[i]);
    }
}
```

We continued to use array notation within the function. If desired, we could have used pointer notation in the function:

```
void displayArray(int* arr, int size) {
    for (int i = 0; i < size; i++) {
        printf("%d\n", *(arr+i));
    }
}
```

If we had used array notation to declare the function, we could have still used pointer notation in the function's body:

```
void displayArray(int arr[], int size) {
    for (int i = 0; i < size; i++) {
        printf("%d\n", *(arr+i));
    }
}
```

Using a One-Dimensional Array of Pointers

In this section, we will examine the key aspects of using an array of pointers by using an array of pointers to integer. Examples of array of pointers can also be found in:

- "Using an Array of Function Pointers" on page 76, where we use an array of function pointers;
- "How Memory Is Allocated for a Structure" on page 135, where an array of structures is used; and
- "Passing Arguments to an Application" on page 125, where the argv array is handled.

The purpose of this section is to set the stage for later examples by illustrating the essence of the approach. The following sequence declares an array of integer pointers, allocates memory for each element, and initializes this memory to the array's index:

```
int* arr[5];
for(int i=0; i<5; i++) {
    arr[i] = (int*)malloc(sizeof(int));
    *arr[i] = i;
}
```

If this array was displayed, the numbers 0 through 4 would be printed. We used arr[i] to reference the pointer and *arr[i] to assign a value to the location referenced by the pointer. Do not let the use of array notation confuse you. Since arr was declared as an array of pointers, arr[i] returns an address. When we dereference a pointer such as *arr[i], we get the contents at that address.

We could have used the following equivalent pointer notation for the loop's body:

```
*(arr+i) = (int*)malloc(sizeof(int));
**(arr+i) = i;
```

This notation is harder to follow, but understanding it will further your C expertise. We are using two levels of indirection in the second statement. Mastery of this type of notation will separate you from the less experienced C programmers.

The subexpression (arr+i) represents the address of the array's ith element. We need to modify the content of this address so we use the subexpression *(arr+i). The allocated memory is assigned to this location in the first statement. Dereferencing this subexpression a second time, as we do in the second statement, returns the allocated memory's location. We then assign the variable i to it. Figure 4-9 illustrates how memory is allocated.

For example, arr[1] is located at address 104. The expression (arr+1) will give us 104. Using *(arr+1) gives us its content. In this example, it is the pointer 504. Dereferencing this a second time using **(arr+1) gives us the contents of 504, which is a 1.

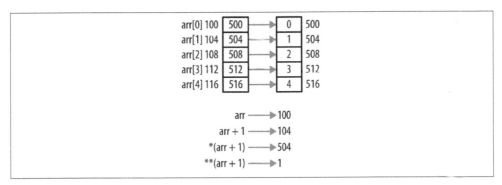

Figure 4-9. Array of pointers

Example expressions are listed in Table 4-3. Reading pointer expression from left to right and not ignoring parentheses can help in understanding how they work.

Table 4-3. Array of pointers expressions

Expression	Value
*arr[0]	0
**arr	0
**(arr+1)	1
arr[0][0]	0
arr[3][0]	3

The first three expressions are similar to those in the previous explanation. The last two are different. The use of a pointer to a pointer notation suggests we are dealing with an array of pointers. In effect, this is what we are doing. If we reexamine Figure 4-9 and pretend each element of arr points to an array of size one, then the last two expressions make sense. What we have is a five-element array of pointers to a series of one-element arrays.

The expression `arr[3][0]` refers to the fourth element of arr and then the first element of the array it points to. The expression `arr[3][1]` does not work because the array the fourth element is pointing to does not have two elements.

This suggests the ability to create jagged arrays. This is indeed possible and is the subject of the section"Jagged Arrays and Pointers" on page 102.

Pointers and Multidimensional Arrays

Parts of multidimensional arrays can be treated as subarrays. For example, each row of a two-dimensional array can be treated as a one-dimensional array. This behavior affects how we use pointers when dealing with multidimensional arrays.

To illustrate this behavior, we create a two-dimensional array and initialize it as follows:

```
int matrix[2][5] = {{1,2,3,4,5},{6,7,8,9,10}};
```

The addresses and their corresponding values are then displayed:

```
for(int i=0; i<2; i++) {
    for(int j=0; j<5; j++) {
        printf("matrix[%d][%d]  Address: %p  Value: %d\n",
                i, j, &matrix[i][j], matrix[i][j]);
    }
}
```

The output follows:

```
matrix[0][0]  Address: 100  Value: 1
matrix[0][1]  Address: 104  Value: 2
matrix[0][2]  Address: 108  Value: 3
matrix[0][3]  Address: 112  Value: 4
matrix[0][4]  Address: 116  Value: 5
matrix[1][0]  Address: 120  Value: 6
matrix[1][1]  Address: 124  Value: 7
matrix[1][2]  Address: 128  Value: 8
matrix[1][3]  Address: 132  Value: 9
matrix[1][4]  Address: 136  Value: 10
```

The array is stored in row-column order. That is, the first row is stored sequentially in memory followed by the second row. The memory allocation is illustrated in Figure 4-10.

We can declare a pointer for use with this array as follows:

```
int (*pmatrix)[5] = matrix;
```

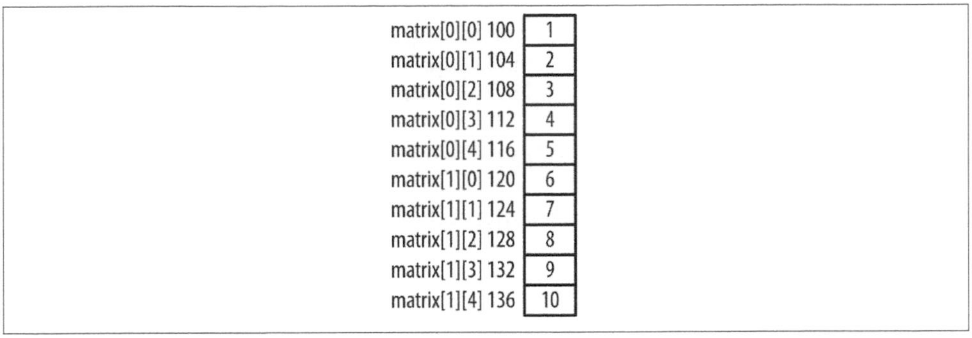

```
matrix[0][0] 100    1
matrix[0][1] 104    2
matrix[0][2] 108    3
matrix[0][3] 112    4
matrix[0][4] 116    5
matrix[1][0] 120    6
matrix[1][1] 124    7
matrix[1][2] 128    8
matrix[1][3] 132    9
matrix[1][4] 136   10
```

Figure 4-10. Two-dimensional array memory allocation

The expression, (*pmatrix), declares a pointer to an array. Combined with the rest of the declaration, pmatrix is defined as a pointer to a two-dimensional array of integers with five elements per column. If we had left the parentheses off, we would have declared a five-element array of pointers to integers. The size of the first dimension is 2 since we know the dimensions of the matrix. If a different size is used to access the array, then the results are unpredictable.

If we want to access the second element, 2, using pointer notation, it might seem reasonable to use the following:

```
printf("%p\n", matrix);
printf("%p\n", matrix + 1);
```

The output follows:

```
100
120
```

The address returned by matrix+1 is not offset by 4 from the beginning of the array. Instead, it is offset by the first row's size, 20 bytes. Using matrix by itself returns the address of the array's first element. Since a two-dimensional array is an array of arrays, we get the address of a five-element integer array. Its size is 20. We can verify this with the following statement, which will display 20:

```
printf("%d\n",sizeof(matrix[0]));   // Displays 20
```

To access the array's second element, we need to add 1 to the first row of the array as follows: *(matrix[0] + 1). The expression, matrix[0], returns the address of the first element of the first row of the array. This address is the address of an array of integers. Thus, when we add one to it, the size of a single integer is added to it, giving us the second element. The output will be 104 and 2.

```
printf("%p  %d\n", matrix[0] + 1, *(matrix[0] + 1));
```

We can graphically depict the array as illustrated in Figure 4-11.

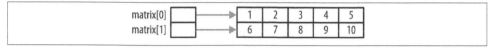

Figure 4-11. Graphically depiction of a two-dimensional array

Two-dimensional array notation can be interpreted as shown in Figure 4-12.

arr[i][j]
address of arr + (i * size of row) + (j * size of element)

Figure 4-12. Two-dimensional array notation

Passing a Multidimensional Array

Passing a multidimensional array to a function can be confusing, especially when pointer notation is used. When passing a multidimensional array, we need to determine whether to use array notation or pointer notation in the function's signature. Another consideration is how to convey the array's shape. By shape, we are referring to the number and size of its dimensions. If we want to use array notation within the function, it is imperative to specify the array's shape. Otherwise, the compiler is unable to use subscripts.

To pass the `matrix` array, use either:

```
void display2DArray(int arr[][5], int rows) {
```

or:

```
void display2DArray(int (*arr)[5], int rows) {
```

In both versions the number of columns is specified. This is needed because the compiler needs to know the number of elements in each row. If this information is not passed, then it is unable to evaluate expressions such as `arr[0][3]` as explained in the section "Pointers and Multidimensional Arrays" on page 94.

In the first version, the expression `arr[]` is an implicit declaration of a pointer to an array. In the second version, the expression `(*arr)` is an explicit declaration of the pointer.

 The following declaration will not work correctly:

```
void display2DArray(int *arr[5], int rows) {
```

While it will not generate a syntax error, the array passed is assumed to be a five-element array of pointers to integers. "Using a One-Dimensional Array of Pointers" on page 92 discusses arrays of pointers.

A simple implementation of this function and invocation follows:

```
void display2DArray(int arr[][5], int rows) {
    for (int i = 0; i<rows; i++) {
        for (int j = 0; j<5; j++) {
            printf("%d", arr[i][j]);
        }
        printf("\n");
    }
}

void main() {
    int matrix[2][5] = {
        {1, 2, 3, 4, 5},
        {6, 7, 8, 9, 10}
    };
    display2DArray(matrix, 2);
}
```

The function does not allocate memory for the array. Only the address is passed. The program stack's state for this call is shown in Figure 4-13.

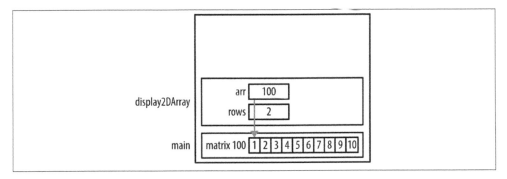

Figure 4-13. Passing multidimensional array

You may encounter a function declared as follows. It is passed a single pointer and the number of rows and columns:

```
void display2DArrayUnknownSize(int *arr, int rows, int cols) {
    for(int i=0; i<rows; i++) {
        for(int j=0; j<cols; j++) {
            printf("%d ", *(arr + (i*cols) + j));
        }
        printf("\n");
    }
}
```

The `printf` statement calculates the address of each element by adding to `arr` the number of elements in the previous row(s), (`i*cols`), and then adding `j` to specify the column. To invoke the function, we can use the following:

```
display2DArrayUnknownSize(&matrix[0][0], 2, 5);
```

Within the function, we cannot use array subscripts as shown below:

```
printf("%d ", arr[i][j]);
```

This is not possible because the pointer is not declared as a two-dimensional array. However, it is possible to use array notation as shown below. We can use a single subscript since it will be interpreted simply as an offset within the array, whereas two subscripts cannot be used because the compiler doesn't know the size of the dimensions:

```
printf("%d ", (arr+i)[j]);
```

The first element's address is passed using &matrix[0][0] instead of matrix. While using matrix will execute correctly, a warning will be generated, indicating incompatible pointer types. The expression &matrix[0][0] is a pointer to an integer, whereas matrix is a pointer to an array of integers.

When passing an array with more than two dimensions, all but the size of the first dimension need to be specified. The following demonstrates a function written to display a three-dimensional array. The last two dimensions are specified in the declaration:

```
void display3DArray(int (*arr)[2][4], int rows) {
    for(int i=0; i<rows; i++) {
        for(int j=0; j<2; j++) {
            printf("{");
            for(int k=0; k<4; k++) {
                printf("%d ", arr[i][j][k]);
            }
            printf("}");
        }
        printf("\n");
    }
}
```

The following code shows the function's invocation:

```
int arr3d[3][2][4] = {
    {{1, 2, 3, 4}, {5, 6, 7, 8}},
    {{9, 10, 11, 12}, {13, 14, 15, 16}},
    {{17, 18, 19, 20}, {21, 22, 23, 24}}
};

display3DArray(arr3d,3);
```

The output follows:

```
{1 2 3 4 }{5 6 7 8 }
{9 10 11 12 }{13 14 15 16 }
{17 18 19 20 }{21 22 23 24 }
```

Allocation of the array's memory is depicted in Figure 4-14.

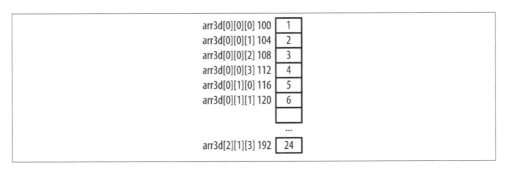

Figure 4-14. Three-dimensional array

The expression `arr3d[1]` refers to the array's second row and is a pointer to a two-dimensional array with two rows and four columns. The expression `arr3d[1][0]` refers to the second row, first column of the array and is a pointer to a one-dimensional array of size 5.

Dynamically Allocating a Two-Dimensional Array

Several issues are involved with dynamically allocating memory for a two-dimensional array, including:

- Whether the array elements need to be contiguous
- Whether the array is jagged

Memory is allocated contiguously when a two-dimensional array is declared as follows:

```
int matrix[2][5] = {{1,2,3,4,5},{6,7,8,9,10}};
```

However, when we use a function such as `malloc` to create a two-dimensional array, there are variations in how memory can be allocated. Since a two-dimensional array can be treated as an array of arrays, there is no reason the "inner" arrays need to be contiguous. When array subscripts are used with such an array, the array's noncontiguous nature is handled transparently.

 Whether or not it is contiguous can affect other operations, such as copying a block of memory. Multiple copies may be required if the memory is not contiguous.

Allocating Potentially Noncontiguous Memory

The following illustrates one way of allocating a two-dimensional array where the allocated memory is not guaranteed to be contiguous. First, the "outer" array is allocated and then each row is allocated using separate `malloc` statements:

```
int rows = 2;
int columns = 5;

int **matrix = (int **) malloc(rows * sizeof(int *));

for (int i = 0; i < rows; i++) {
    matrix[i] = (int *) malloc(columns * sizeof(int));
}
```

Since separate `malloc` calls were used, the allocated memory is not guaranteed to be contiguous. This is illustrated in Figure 4-15.

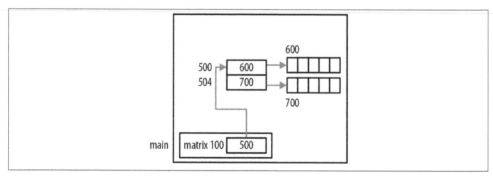

Figure 4-15. Noncontiguous allocation

The actual allocation depends on the heap manager and the heap's state. It may well be contiguous.

Allocating Contiguous Memory

We will present two approaches for allocating contiguous memory for a two-dimensional array. The first technique allocates the "outer" array first and then all of the memory for the rows. The second technique allocates all of the memory at once.

The first technique is illustrated in the following sequence. The first `malloc` allocates an array of pointers to integers. Each element will be used to hold a pointer to a row. This is the block allocated at address 500 in Figure 4-16. The second `malloc` allocates memory for all of the elements of the array at location 600. In the `for` loop, each element of the first array is assigned a portion of the memory allocated by the second `malloc`:

```
int rows = 2;
int columns = 5;
int **matrix = (int **) malloc(rows * sizeof(int *));
matrix[0] = (int *) malloc(rows * columns * sizeof(int));
for (int i = 1; i < rows; i++)
    matrix[i] = matrix[0] + i * columns;
```

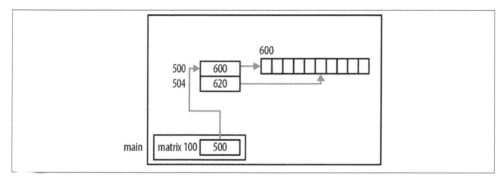

Figure 4-16. Contiguous allocation with two malloc calls

Technically, the memory for the first array may be separated from the memory for the array's "body." However, a contiguous region of memory is allocated for the body.

In the second technique shown below, all of the memory for the array is allocated at one time:

```
int *matrix = (int *)malloc(rows * columns * sizeof(int));
```

This allocation is illustrated in Figure 4-17.

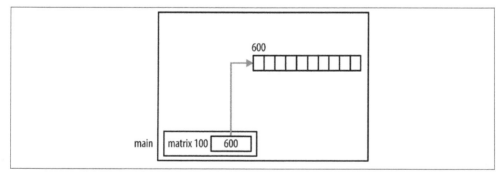

Figure 4-17. Contiguous allocation with a single malloc call

When the array is referenced later in code, array subscripts cannot be used. Instead, indexes into the array need to be calculated manually, as illustrated in the following code sequence. Each array element is initialized to the product of its indexes:

```
    for (int i = 0; i < rows; i++) {
        for (int j = 0; j < columns; j++) {
            *(matrix + (i*columns) + j) = i*j;
        }
    }
```

Array subscripts cannot be used because we have lost the shape information needed by the compiler to permit subscripts. This concept is explained in the section "Passing a Multidimensional Array" on page 96.

This approach has limited use in the real world, but it does illustrate the relationship between the concept of a two-dimensional array and the one-dimensional nature of main memory. The more convenient two-dimensional array notation makes this mapping transparent and easier to use.

We have demonstrated two general approaches for allocating contiguous memory for a two-dimensional array. The approach to use depends on the needs of the application. However, the last approach generates a single block of memory for the "entire" array.

Jagged Arrays and Pointers

A jagged array is a two-dimensional array possessing a different number of columns for each row. Conceptually, this is illustrated in Figure 4-18, where the array has three rows with a varying number of columns per row.

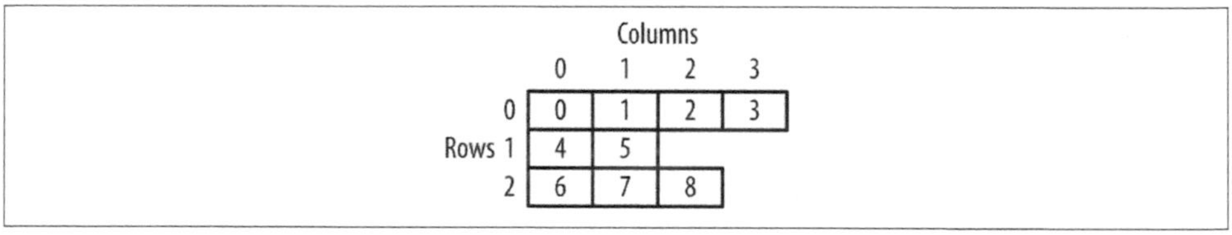

Figure 4-18. Jagged array

Before we learn how to create such an array, let's examine a two-dimensional array created using *compound literals*. A compound literal is a C construct that consists of what appears to be a cast operator followed by an initializer list enclosed in braces. An example of a compound literal follows for both a constant integer and an array of integers. These would be used as part of a declaration:

```
(const int) {100}
(int[3]) {10, 20, 30}
```

In the following declaration, we create the array arr1 by declaring it as an array of pointers to an integer and using a block statement of compound literals to initialize it:

```
int (*(arr1[])) = {
    (int[]) {0, 1, 2},
```

```
        (int[]) {3, 4, 5},
        (int[]) {6, 7, 8}};
```

This array has three rows and three columns. The array's elements are initialized with the value 0 through 8 in row column order. Figure 4-19 depicts how memory is laid out for this array.

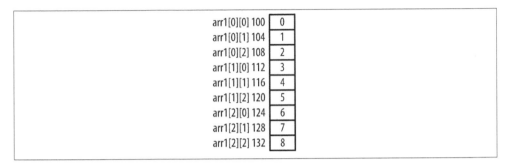

Figure 4-19. Two-dimensional array

The following sequence displays the addresses and values of each array element:

```
for(int j=0; j<3; j++) {
    for(int i=0; i<3; i++) {
        printf("arr1[%d][%d]  Address: %p  Value: %d\n",
                j, i, &arr1[j][i], arr1[j][i]);
    }
    printf("\n");
}
```

When executed, we will get the following output:

```
arr1[0][0]  Address: 0x100  Value: 0
arr1[0][1]  Address: 0x104  Value: 1
arr1[0][2]  Address: 0x108  Value: 2

arr1[1][0]  Address: 0x112  Value: 3
arr1[1][1]  Address: 0x116  Value: 4
arr1[1][2]  Address: 0x120  Value: 5

arr1[2][0]  Address: 0x124  Value: 6
arr1[2][1]  Address: 0x128  Value: 7
arr1[2][2]  Address: 0x132  Value: 8
```

This declaration can be modified slightly to create a jagged array as depicted in Figure 4-18. The array declaration follows:

```
int (*(arr2[])) = {
    (int[]) {0, 1, 2, 3},
    (int[]) {4, 5},
    (int[]) {6, 7, 8}};
```

We used three compound literals to declare the jagged array. The array's elements are initialized in row-column order starting with a value of zero. The next sequence will display the array to verify its creation. The sequence required three for loops because each row had a different number of columns:

```
int row = 0;
for(int i=0; i<4; i++) {
    printf("layer1[%d][%d]  Address: %p  Value: %d\n",
           row, i, &arr2[row][i], arr2[row][i]);
}
printf("\n");

row = 1;
for(int i=0; i<2; i++) {
    printf("layer1[%d][%d]  Address: %p  Value: %d\n",
           row, i, &arr2[row][i], arr2[row][i]);
}
printf("\n");

row = 2;
for(int i=0; i<3; i++) {
    printf("layer1[%d][%d]  Address: %p  Value: %d\n",
           row, i, &arr2[row][i], arr2[row][i]);
}
printf("\n");
```

The output of this sequence follows:

```
arr2[0][0]  Address: 0x000100  Value: 0
arr2[0][1]  Address: 0x000104  Value: 1
arr2[0][2]  Address: 0x000108  Value: 2
arr2[0][3]  Address: 0x000112  Value: 3

arr2[1][0]  Address: 0x000116  Value: 4
arr2[1][1]  Address: 0x000120  Value: 5

arr2[2][0]  Address: 0x000124  Value: 6
arr2[2][1]  Address: 0x000128  Value: 7
arr2[2][2]  Address: 0x000132  Value: 8
```

Figure 4-20 depicts how memory is laid out for this array.

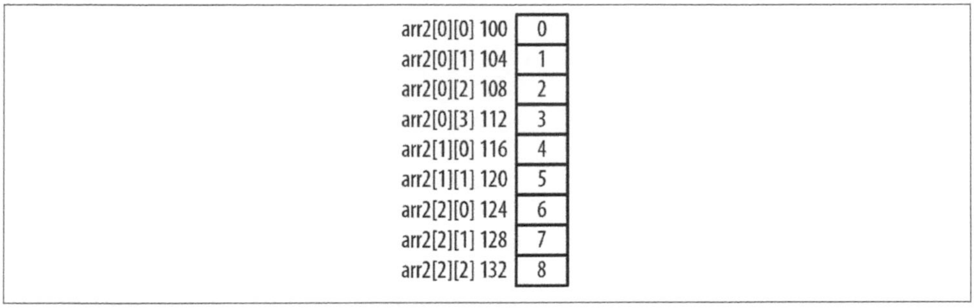

```
arr2[0][0] 100   0
arr2[0][1] 104   1
arr2[0][2] 108   2
arr2[0][3] 112   3
arr2[1][0] 116   4
arr2[1][1] 120   5
arr2[2][0] 124   6
arr2[2][1] 128   7
arr2[2][2] 132   8
```

Figure 4-20. Jagged array memory allocation

In these examples, we used array notation as opposed to pointer notation when accessing the array's contents. This made it somewhat easier to see and understand. However, pointer notation would have worked as well.

Compound literals are useful in creating jagged arrays. However, accessing elements of a jagged array can be awkward, as demonstrated with the previous three for loops. This example can be simplified if a separate array is used to maintain the size of each column. While you can create jagged arrays in C, it may not be worth the effort.

Summary

We started with a quick review of arrays and then examined the similarities and differences between array and pointer notation. Arrays can be created using `malloc` type functions. These type of functions provide more flexibility than afforded by traditional array declaration. We saw how we can use the `realloc` function to change the amount of memory allocated for an array.

Dynamically allocating memory for an array can present challenges. In the case with two or more dimensional arrays, we have to be careful to make sure the array is allocated in contiguous memory.

We also explored the problems that can occur when passing and returning arrays. Passing the array's size to a function is normally required so the function can properly handle the array. We also examined how to create jagged arrays in C.

CHAPTER 5

Pointers and Strings

Strings can be allocated to different regions of memory and pointers are commonly used to support string operations. Pointers support the dynamic allocation of strings and passing strings to a function. A good understanding of pointers and their use with strings enables programmers to develop valid and efficient applications.

Strings are a common component of many applications and are a complex topic. In this chapter, we will explore the various ways of declaring and initializing strings. We will examine the use of literal pools in C applications and their impact. In addition, we will look at common string operations, such as comparing, copying, and concatenating strings.

Strings are regularly passed and returned to functions as pointers to char. When we pass a string, we can do so either as a pointer to a char or a pointer to a constant char. The latter approach protects the string from modification within the function. Many examples used in this chapter provide additional illustrations of the concepts developed in the function chapter. They differ as they do not need to pass their size to a function.

A string may also be returned from a function to fulfill a request. This string may be passed to the function to be modified or allocated from within the function. We could also return a statically allocated string. Each of these approaches will be examined.

We will also examine the use of function pointers and how they can assist sorting operations. Understanding how pointers work in these situations is the primary focus of this chapter.

String Fundamentals

A string is a sequence of characters terminated with the ASCII NUL character. The ASCII character NUL is represented as \0. Strings are commonly stored in arrays or in memory allocated from the heap. However, not all arrays of characters are strings. An array of char may not contain the NUL character. Arrays of char have been used to represent smaller integer units, such as boolean, to conserve memory space in an application.

There are two types of strings in C:

Byte string
> Consists of a sequence of char data type

Wide string
> Consists of a sequence of wchar_t data type

The wchar_t data type is used for wide characters and may be either 16 or 32 bits in width. Both of these strings are terminated by the NUL character. Byte string functions are found in the *string.h* file. Wide string functions are found in the *wchar.h* file. Unless otherwise noted, we will be using byte strings in this chapter. Wide chars were created to support non-Latin character sets and are useful in applications that support foreign languages.

The length of a string is the number of characters in the string. This does not include the NUL character. When memory is allocated for a string, remember to allocate enough memory for all of the characters plus the NUL character.

 Remember that NULL and NUL are different. NULL is used as a special pointer and is typically defined as ((void*)0). NUL is a char and is defined as '\0'. They should not be used interchangeably.

Character constants are character sequences enclosed in single quotes. Normally, they consist of a single character but can contain more than one character, as found with escape sequences. In C, they are of type int. This is demonstrated as follows:

```
printf("%d\n",sizeof(char));
printf("%d\n",sizeof('a'));
```

When executed, the size of char will be 1 while the character literal's size will be 4. This anomaly is an artifact of the language design.

String Declaration

String declarations are supported in one of three ways: either as a literal, as an array of characters, or using a pointer to a character. The string literal is a sequence of characters enclosed in double quotes. String literals are frequently used for initialization purposes. They are located in a string literal pool discussed in the next section.

String literals are not to be confused with characters enclosed in single quotes—these are character literals. As we will see in later sections, when used in place of string literals, character literals can cause problems.

An array of characters is illustrated below where we declare a header array whose size may hold up to 31 characters. Since a string requires the NUL termination character, an array declared to have 32 characters can only use 31 elements for the actual string's text. The string's location depends on where the declaration is placed. We will explore this issue in the section "String Initialization" on page 110.

```
char header[32];
```

A pointer to a character is illustrated below. Since it has not been initialized, it does not reference a string. The string's length and location are not specified at this time.

```
char *header;
```

The String Literal Pool

When literals are defined they are frequently assigned to a literal pool. This area of memory holds the character sequences making up a string. When a literal is used more than once, there is normally only a single copy of the string in the string literal pool. This will reduce the amount of space needed for the application. Since a literal is normally considered to be immutable, it does not hurt to have a single copy of it. However, it is not a good practice to assume there will only be a single copy or that literals are immutable. Most compilers provide an option to turn off string pooling. When this happens, literals may be duplicated, each having their own address.

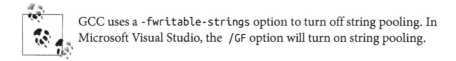

GCC uses a -fwritable-strings option to turn off string pooling. In Microsoft Visual Studio, the /GF option will turn on string pooling.

Figure 5-1 illustrates how memory may be allocated for a literal pool.

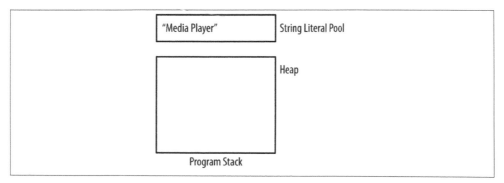

Figure 5-1. String literal pool

String literals are frequently allocated to read-only memory. This makes them immutable. It doesn't matter where a string literal is used or whether it is global, static, or local. In this sense, string literals do not have scope.

When a string literal is not a constant

In most compilers, a string literal is treated as a constant. It is not possible to modify the string. However, in some compilers, such as GCC, modification of the string literal is possible. Consider the following example:

```
char *tabHeader  = "Sound";
*tabHeader = 'L';
printf("%s\n",tabHeader);   // Displays "Lound"
```

This will modify the literal to "Lound." Normally, this is not desirable and should be avoided. Making the variable a constant as follows will provide a partial solution to this problem. Any attempt to modify the string will result in a compile-time error.

```
const char *tabHeader  = "Sound";
```

String Initialization

When we initialize a string, the approach we use depends on whether the variable is declared as an array of characters or as a pointer to a character. The memory used for a string will be either an array or a memory pointed to by a pointer. When a string is initialized, we can use a string literal or a series of characters, or obtain the characters from a different source such as standard input. We will examine these approaches.

Initializing an array of char

An array of char can be initialized using the initialization operator. In the following example, a header array is initialized to the character contained in a string literal:

```
char header[] = "Media Player";
```

Since the literal "Media Player" is 12 characters in length, 13 bytes are required to represent the literal. The array is allocated 13 bytes to hold the string. The initialization will copy these characters to the array terminated by the NUL character, as illustrated in Figure 5-2, assuming the declaration is located in the main function.

An array can also be initialized using strcpy function, which is discussed in detail in the section "Copying Strings" on page 116. In the following sequence, the string literal is copied to the array.

```
char header[13];
strcpy(header,"Media Player");
```

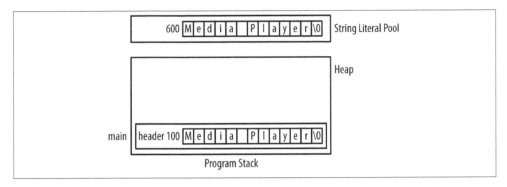

Figure 5-2. Initializing an array of char

A more tedious technique assigns individual characters as follows:

```
header[0] = 'M';
header[1] = 'e';
    ...
header[12] = '\0';
```

 The following assignment is invalid. We cannot assign the address of a string literal to an array name.

```
char header2[];
header2 = "Media Player";
```

Initializing a pointer to a char

Using dynamic memory allocation provides flexibility and potentially allows the memory to stay around longer. The following declaration will be used to illustrate this technique:

```
char *header;
```

A common way to initialize this string is to use the `malloc` and `strcpy` functions to allocate and copy a literal to the string, as illustrated below:

```
char *header = (char*) malloc(strlen("Media Player")+1);
strcpy(header,"Media Player");
```

Assuming that the code is located in the main function, Figure 5-3 shows the state of the program stack.

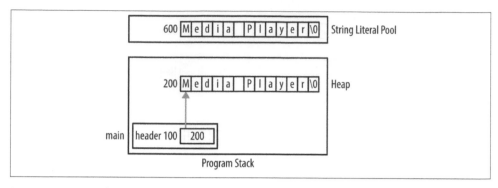

Figure 5-3. Initializing a pointer to a char

In the previous use of the `malloc` function, we used the `strlen` function with a string literal argument. We could have declared its size explicitly as shown below:

```
char *header = (char*) malloc(13);
```

 When determining the length of a string to be used with the `malloc` function:

- Always remember to add one for the NUL terminator.
- Don't use `sizeof` operator. Instead, use the `strlen` function to determine the length of an existing string. The `sizeof` operator will return the size of an array or pointer, not the length of the string.

Instead of using a string literal and `strcpy` function to initialize the string, we can use the following:

```
*(header + 0) = 'M';
*(header + 1) = 'e';
    ...
*(header + 12) = '\0';
```

The address of a string literal can be assigned directly to a character pointer as shown below. However, this does not create a new copy of the string as illustrated in Figure 5-4:

```
char *header = "Media Player";
```

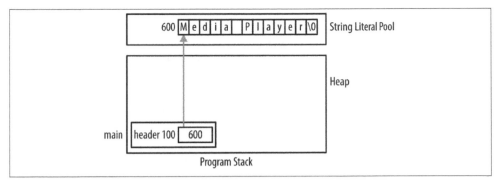

Figure 5-4. Copying a string literal's address to a pointer

Attempting to initialize a pointer to a char with a character literal will not work. Since a character literal is of type int, we would be trying to assign an integer to a character pointer. This will frequently cause the application to terminate when the pointer is dereferenced:

```
char* prefix = '+';    // Illegal
```

A valid approach using the malloc function follows:

```
prefix = (char*)malloc(2);
*prefix = '+';
*(prefix+1) = 0;
```

Initializing a string from standard input

A string can also be initialized from some external source such as standard input. However, potential initialization errors can occur when reading in a string from standard input, as shown below. The problem exists because we have not assigned memory to the command variable before attempting to use it:

```
char *command;
printf("Enter a Command: ");
scanf("%s",command);
```

To address this problem, we should first allocate memory for the pointer or use a fixed size array instead of a pointer. However, the user may enter more data than can be held by these approaches. A more robust approach is illustrated in Chapter 4.

Summary of string placement

Strings can be allocated in several potential locations. The following example illustrates possible variations with Figure 5-5 illustrates how these strings are laid out in memory:

```
char* globalHeader = "Chapter";
char globalArrayHeader[] = "Chapter";

void displayHeader() {
    static char* staticHeader = "Chapter";
```

```
    char* localHeader = "Chapter";
    static char staticArrayHeader[] = "Chapter";
    char localArrayHeader[] = "Chapter";
    char* heapHeader = (char*)malloc(strlen("Chapter")+1);
    strcpy(heapHeader,"Chapter");
}
```

Knowing where a string is located is useful when attempting to understand how a program works and when using pointers to access the strings. A string's location determines how long it will persist and which parts of an application can access it. For example, strings allocated to global memory will always be available and are accessible by multiple functions. Static strings will always be available but are accessible only to their defining function. Strings allocated to the heap will persist until they are released and may be used in multiple functions. Understanding these issues allows you to make informed decisions.

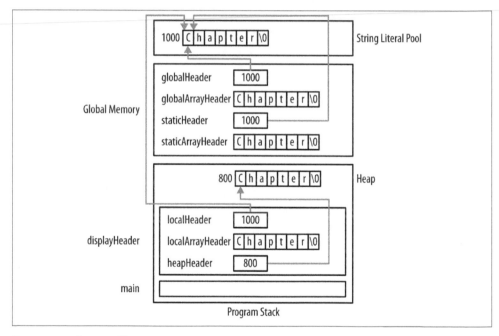

Figure 5-5. String allocation in memory

Standard String Operations

In this section, we will examine the use of pointers in common string operations. This includes comparing, copying, and concatenating strings.

Comparing Strings

String comparisons can be an integral part of an application. We will examine the details of how string comparisons are made, as incorrect comparisons can result in misleading or invalid results. Understanding how comparisons are made will help you avoid incorrect operations. This understanding will transfer to similar situations.

The standard way to compare strings is to use the strcmp function. Its prototype follows:

```
int strcmp(const char *s1, const char *s2);
```

Both of the strings being compared are passed as pointers to constant chars. This allows us to use the function without fear of it modifying the strings passed. This function returns one of three values:

Negative
    If s1 precedes s2 lexicographically (alphabetically)

Zero
    If the two strings are equal

Positive
    If s1 follows s2 lexicographically

The positive and negative return values are useful for sorting strings in alphabetical order. The use of this function to test equality is illustrated below. The user's entry will be stored in command. This is then compared to the literal string:

```
char command[16];

printf("Enter a Command: ");
scanf("%s", command);
if (strcmp(command, "Quit") == 0) {
    printf("The command was Quit");
} else {
    printf("The command was not Quit");
}
```

Memory for this example is allocated as shown in Figure 5-6.

There are a couple of incorrect ways to compare two strings. The first approach shown below attempts to use the assignment operator to perform the comparison:

```
char command[16];

printf("Enter a Command: ");
scanf("%s",command);
if(command = "Quit") {
    ...
```

First, it does not perform a comparison, and second, this will result in a syntax error message complaining about incompatible types. We cannot assign the address of a string

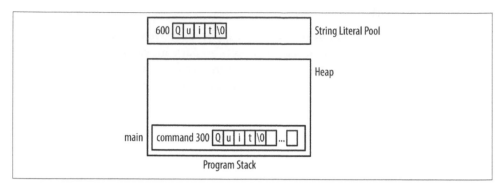

Figure 5-6. strcmp example

literal to the array name. In this example, we tried to assign the string literal's address, 600, to command. Since command is an array, it is not possible to assign a value to this variable without using array subscripts.

The second approach is to use the equality operator:

```
char command[16];

printf("Enter a Command: ");
scanf("%s",command);
if(command == "Quit") {
    ...
```

This should evaluate false since we are comparing the address of command, 300, with the string literal's address, 600. The equality operator compares the addresses, not what is stored at the addresses. Using an array name or a string literal by themselves will return their addresses.

Copying Strings

Copying strings is a common operation and is normally accomplished using the strcpy function whose prototype follows:

```
char* strcpy(char *s1, const char *s2);
```

In this section, we will cover the basic copying process and identify common pitfalls. We will assume there is a need to copy an existing string to a new dynamically allocated buffer, though we could also have used an array of characters.

A common application is to read in a series of strings and store each of them in an array using a minimum amount of memory. This can be accomplished by creating an array sized to handle the largest string that the user might enter and then reading it into this array. On the basis of the string read in, we can then allocate just the right amount of memory. The basic approach is to:

---

1. Read in the string using a large array of char

2. Use malloc to allocate just the right amount of memory

3. Use strcpy to copy the string into the dynamically allocated memory

The following sequence illustrates this technique. The names array will hold pointers to each name read in. The count variable specifies the next available array element. The name array is used to hold a string that is read in and is reused for each name read. The malloc function allocates the memory needed for each string and is assigned to the next available element of names. The name is then copied into the allocated memory:

```
char name[32];
char *names[30];
size_t count = 0;

printf("Enter a name: ");
scanf("%s",name);
names[count] = (char*)malloc(strlen(name)+1);
strcpy(names[count],name);
count++;
```

We can repeat the operation within a loop, incrementing count with each iteration. Figure 5-7 illustrates how memory is laid out for this process after reading in a single name: "Sam."

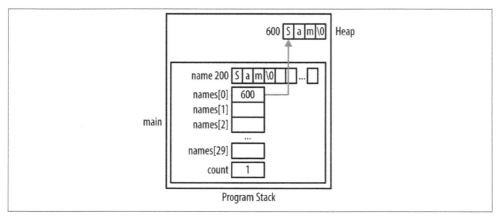

Figure 5-7. Copying a string

Two pointers can reference the same string. When two pointers reference the same location, this is called *aliasing*. This topic is covered in Chapter 8. While this is not necessarily a problem, realize that the assignment of one pointer to another does not result in the string being copied. Instead, we simply copied the string's address.

To illustrate this, an array of pointers to page headers is declared below. The page with index 12 is assigned the address of a string literal. Next, the pointer in pageHeaders[12] is copied to pageHeaders[13]. Both of these pointers now reference the same string literal. The pointer is copied, not the string:

```
char *pageHeaders[300];

pageHeaders[12] = "Amorphous Compounds";
pageHeaders[13] = pageHeaders[12];
```

These assignments are illustrated in Figure 5-8.

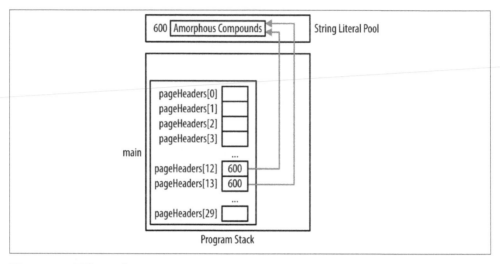

Figure 5-8. Effects of copying pointers

Concatenating Strings

String concatenation involves the merging of two strings. The strcat function is frequently used for this operation. This function takes pointers to the two strings to be concatenated and returns a pointer to the concatenated results. The prototype for the function follows:

```
char *strcat(char *s1, const char *s2);
```

The function concatenates the second string to the end of the first string. The second string is passed as a pointer to a constant char. The function does not allocate memory. This means the first string must be large enough to hold the concatenated results or it may write past the end of the string, resulting in unpredictable behavior. The return value of the function is the same address as its first argument. This can be convenient in some situations such as when the function is used as an argument of the printf function.

To illustrate the use of this function, we will combine two error message strings. The first one is a prefix and the second one is a specific error message. As shown below, we first need to allocate enough memory for both strings in a buffer, then copy the first string to the buffer, and finally concatenate the second string with the buffer:

```
char* error = "ERROR: ";
char* errorMessage = "Not enough memory";

char* buffer = (char*)malloc(strlen(error)+strlen(errorMessage)+1);
strcpy(buffer,error);
strcat(buffer, errorMessage);

printf("%s\n", buffer);
printf("%s\n", error);
printf("%s\n", errorMessage);
```

We added one to the malloc function's argument to accommodate the NUL character. If we assume the first literal immediately precedes the second literal in memory, the output of this sequence will be as follows. Figure 5-9 illustrates how memory is allocated:

```
ERROR: Not enough memory
ERROR:
Not enough memory
```

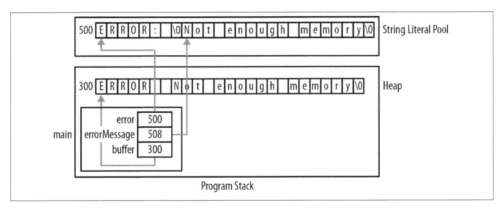

Figure 5-9. Correct copy operation

If we had not allocated a separate memory location for the concatenated string, we would overwrite the first string. This is illustrated in the following example, where a buffer is not used. We also assume the first literal immediately precedes the second literal in memory:

```
char* error = "ERROR: ";
char* errorMessage = "Not enough memory";

strcat(error, errorMessage);
```

```
    printf("%s\n", error);
    printf("%s\n", errorMessage);
```

The output of this sequence follows:

```
ERROR: Not enough memory
ot enough memory
```

The `errorMessage` string has been shifted one character to the left. This is because the resulting concatenated string is written over `errorMessage`. Since the literal "Not enough memory" follows the first literal, the second literal is overwritten. This is illustrated in Figure 5-10, where the literal pool's state is displayed before and after the copy operation.

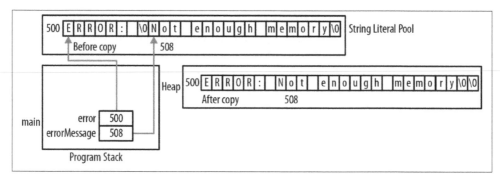

Figure 5-10. Improper string copy operation

We could have used a `char` array instead of a pointer for the messages, as shown below. However, this will not always work:

```
    char error[] = "ERROR: ";
    char errorMessage[] = "Not enough memory";
```

If we used the following `strcpy` call, we would get a syntax error. This is because we are attempting to assign the pointer returned by the function to the name of an array. This type of operation is illegal:

```
    error = strcat(error, errorMessage);
```

If we remove the assignment, as follows, we would likely get a memory access violation, since the copy operation is overwriting a part of the stack frame. This assumes the array declarations are in a function, as illustrated in Figure 5-11. Whether the source strings are stored in the string literal pool or on the stack frame, they should not be used to directly hold the concatenated result. Always allocate dedicated memory for the concatenation.

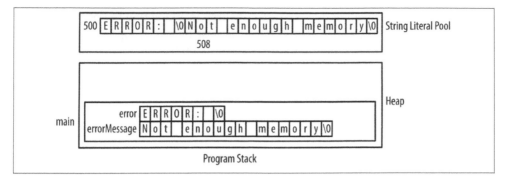

Figure 5-11. Overwriting the stack frame

Another simple mistake made when concatenating strings is using a character literal instead of a string literal. In the following example, we concatenate a string to a path string. This will work as expected:

```
char path[] = "C:";
char* currentPath = (char*) malloc(strlen(path) + 2);
strcpy(currentPath,path);
strcat(currentPath, "\\");
```

We add two to the string length in the `malloc` call because we need space for the extra character and the NUL character. We are concatenating a single character, the backslash, since we used an escape sequence in the string literal.

However, if we used a character literal instead, as shown below, we will get a runtime error when the second argument is mistakenly interpreted as the address of a `char`:

```
currentPath = strcat(path,'\\');
```

Passing Strings

Passing a string is simple enough. In the function call, use an expression that evaluates to the address of a `char`. In the parameter list, declare the parameter as a pointer to a `char`. The interesting issues occur when using the string within the function. We will first examine how to pass a simple string in the first two subsections and then how to pass a string requiring initialization in the third section. Passing strings as arguments to an application is covered in the section "Passing Arguments to an Application" on page 125.

Passing a Simple String

There are several ways of passing the address of a string to a function, depending on how the string is declared. In this section, we will demonstrate these techniques using a function that mimics the `strlen` function as implemented below. We used parentheses to force the post increment operator to execute first, incrementing the pointer. While the use of parentheses is not required, since the post-increment operator has higher precedence than the dereference operator, it makes the intent clear:

```
size_t stringLength(char* string) {
    size_t length = 0;
    while(*(string++)) {
        length++;
    }
    return length;
}
```

 The string should actually be passed as a pointer to a constant char, as discussed in the section "Passing a Pointer to a Constant char" on page 123.

Let's start with the following declarations:

```
char simpleArray[] = "simple string";
char *simplePtr = (char*)malloc(strlen("simple string")+1);
strcpy(simplePtr, "simple string");
```

To invoke the function with the pointer, we simply use the pointer's name:

```
printf("%d\n",stringLength(simplePtr));
```

To invoke the function using the array, we have three choices, as shown below. In the first statement, we use the array's name. This will return its address. In the second statement, the address-of operator is used explicitly. While this will work, we are passing a pointer to a pointer to a char instead of a pointer to a char, which will generate a warning. In the third statement, we used the address-of operator with the array's first element. While this works, it is somewhat verbose:

```
printf("%d\n",stringLength(simpleArray));
printf("%d\n",stringLength(&simpleArray));
printf("%d\n",stringLength(&simpleArray[0]));
```

Figure 5-12 illustrates how memory will be allocated for the stringLength function.

Now let's turn our attention to how we declare the formal parameter. In the previous implementation of stringLength, we declared the parameter as a pointer to a char. We could have also used array notation as shown below:

```
size_t stringLength(char string[]) { ... }
```

The function's body will stay the same. This change will have no effect on how the function is invoked or its behavior.

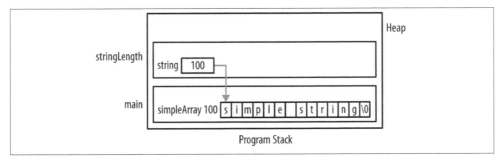

Figure 5-12. Passing a string

Passing a Pointer to a Constant char

Passing a pointer to a string as a constant char is a very common and useful technique. It passes the string using a pointer, and at the same time prevents the string being passed from being modified. A better implementation of the stringLength function developed in the section "Passing Strings" on page 121 incorporates this declaration as follows:

```
size_t stringLength(const char* string) {
    size_t length = 0;
    while(*(string++)) {
        length++;
    }
    return length;
}
```

If we attempt to modify the original string as follows, then a compile-time error message will be generated:

```
size_t stringLength(const char* string) {
    ...
    *string = 'A';
    ...
}
```

Passing a String to Be Initialized

There are situations where we want a function to return a string initialized by the function. For example, we may want to pass information about a part, such as its name and quantity, and then have a formatted string representing this information returned. By keeping the formatting process in a function we can reuse it in different sections of our program.

However, we need to decide whether we want to pass the function an empty buffer to be filled and returned by the function, or whether the buffer should be dynamically allocated by the function and then returned to us.

When a buffer is passed:

- The buffer's address and its size must be passed
- The caller is responsible for deallocating the buffer
- The function normally returns a pointer to this buffer

This approach keeps the buffer's allocation and deallocation responsibility with the caller. Returning a pointer to the buffer is common, even if it is unnecessary, as typified by `strcpy` and similar functions. The following `format` function illustrates this approach:

```
char* format(char *buffer, size_t size,
        const char* name, size_t quantity, size_t weight) {
    snprintf(buffer, size, "Item: %s  Quantity: %u  Weight: %u",
            name, quantity, weight);
    return buffer;
}
```

The `snprintf` function was used as a simple way of formatting the string. This function writes to the buffer provided by the first parameter. The second argument specifies the buffer's size. This function will not write past the end of the buffer. Otherwise, the function behaves the same way as `printf`.

The following demonstrates the use of the function:

```
printf("%s\n",format(buffer,sizeof(buffer),"Axle",25,45));
```

The output of this sequence is as follows:

```
Item: Axle  Quantity: 25  Weight: 45
```

By returning a pointer to `buffer`, we are able to use the function as a parameter of the `printf` function.

An alternative to this approach is to pass NULL as the buffer's address. This implies the caller does not want to provide the buffer or is unsure how large the buffer should be. This version of the function can be implemented as follows. When length is calculated the subexpression `10 + 10` represents the largest width anticipated for the quantity and weight. The one allows space for the NUL termination character:

```
char* format(char *buffer, size_t size,
        const char* name, size_t quantity, size_t weight) {

    char *formatString = "Item: %s  Quantity: %u  Weight: %u";
    size_t formatStringLength = strlen(formatString)-6;
    size_t nameLength = strlen(name);
    size_t length = formatStringLength + nameLength +
            10 + 10 + 1;

    if(buffer == NULL) {
```

```
        buffer = (char*)malloc(length);
        size = length;
    }
    snprintf(buffer, size, formatString, name, quantity, weight);
    return buffer;
}
```

The function variation to use depends on the needs of the application. The chief draw-back of the second approach is that the caller is now responsible for freeing the memory allocated. The caller needs to be fully aware of how this function should be used; otherwise, a memory leak can easily occur.

Passing Arguments to an Application

The main function is normally the first function in an application to be executed. With console-based programs it is common to pass information to the program to enable or otherwise control the application's behavior. These parameters may be used to specify which files to process or to configure the application's output. For example, the ls Linux command will list the files in the current directory based on parameters used with the command.

C supports command line arguments using the traditionally named argc and argv parameters. The first parameter, argc, is an integer that indicates how many parameters are passed. At least one parameter is always passed. This parameter is the name of the executable. The second parameter, argv, is normally viewed as a one-dimensional array of string pointers. Each pointer references a command line argument.

The following main function will simply list its arguments one per line. In this version, argv is declared as a pointer to a pointer to a char:

```
int main(int argc, char** argv) {
    for(int i=0; i<argc; i++) {
        printf("argv[%d] %s\n",i,argv[i]);
    }
    ...
}
```

The program is executed with the following command line:

```
process.exe -f names.txt limit=12 -verbose
```

The output will be as follows:

```
argv[0] c:/process.exe
argv[1] -f
argv[2] names.txt
argv[3] limit=12
argv[4] -verbose
```

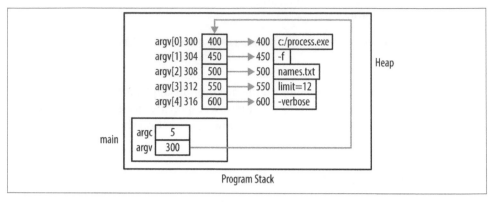

Figure 5-13. Using argc/argv

Each command line parameter is delineated by whitespace. The memory allocated for the program is illustrated in Figure 5-13.

The declaration of `argv` can be simplified as follows:

```
int main(int argc, char* argv[]) {
```

This is equivalent to `char** argv`. A more detailed explanation of this notation is found in "Multiple Levels of Indirection" on page 25.

Returning Strings

When a function returns a string, it returns the address of the string. The main concern is to return a valid string address. To do this, we can return a reference to either:

- A literal
- Dynamically allocated memory
- A local string variable

Returning the Address of a Literal

An example of returning a literal is shown below. An integer code selects from one of four different processing centers. The function's purpose is to return the processing center's name as a string. In this example, it simply returns the literal's address:

```
char* returnALiteral(int code) {
    switch(code) {
        case 100:
            return "Boston Processing Center";
        case 200:
```

```
            return "Denver Processing Center";
        case 300:
            return "Atlanta Processing Center";
        case 400:
            return "San Jose Processing Center";
    }
}
```

This will work fine. Just keep in mind that string literals are not always treated as constants, as discussed in the section "When a string literal is not a constant" on page 110. We can also declare static literals as in the following example. A `subCode` field has been added and selects between different centers. The advantage of this approach is not having to use the same literal in more than one place and possibly introducing errors by mistyping the literal:

```
char* returnAStaticLiteral(int code, int subCode) {
    static char* bpCenter = "Boston Processing Center";
    static char* dpCenter = "Denver Processing Center";
    static char* apCenter = "Atlanta Processing Center";
    static char* sjpCenter = "San Jose Processing Center";

    switch(code) {
        case 100:
            return bpCenter;
        case 135:
            if(subCode <35) {
                return dpCenter;
            } else {
                return bpCenter;
            }
        case 200:
            return dpCenter;
        case 300:
            return apCenter;
        case 400:
            return sjpCenter;
    }
}
```

Returning a pointer to a static string used for multiple purposes can be a problem. Consider the following variation of the `format` function developed in the section "Passing a String to Be Initialized" on page 123. Information about a part is passed to the function and a formatted string representing the string is returned:

```
char* staticFormat(const char* name, size_t quantity, size_t weight) {
    static char buffer[64];  // Assume to be large enough
    sprintf(buffer, "Item: %s  Quantity: %u  Weight: %u",
            name, quantity, weight);
    return buffer;
}
```

The buffer is allocated 64 bytes, which may or may not be enough. For purposes of this example, we will ignore this potential problem. The main problem with this approach is illustrated with the following sequence:

```
char* part1 = staticFormat("Axle",25,45);
char* part2 = staticFormat("Piston",55,5);
printf("%s\n",part1);
printf("%s\n",part2);
```

When executed, we get the following output:

```
Item: Piston  Quantity: 55  Weight: 5
Item: Piston  Quantity: 55  Weight: 5
```

Since the staticFormat method used the same static buffer for both calls, the last call overwrote the first call's results.

Returning the Address of Dynamically Allocated Memory

If a string needs to be returned from a function, the memory for the string can be allocated from the heap and then its address can be returned. We will demonstrate this technique by developing a blanks function. This function returns a string containing a series of blanks representing a "tab," as shown below. The function is passed an integer specifying the tab sequence's length:

```
char* blanks(int number) {
    char* spaces = (char*) malloc(number + 1);
    int i;
    for (i = 0; i<number; i++) {
        spaces[i] = ' ';
    }
    spaces[number] = '\0';
    return spaces;
}


    ...
    char *tmp = blanks(5);
```

The NUL termination character is assigned to the last element of the array indexed by number. Figure 5-14 illustrates the allocation of memory for this example. It shows the application's state just before and after the blanks function returns.

It is the function's caller's responsibility to deallocate the memory returned. Failure to deallocate it when it is no longer needed will result in a memory leak. The following is an example of when a memory leak can occur. The string is used within the printf function and its address is subsequently lost because it was not saved:

```
printf("[%s]\n",blanks(5));
```

A safer approach is demonstrated below:

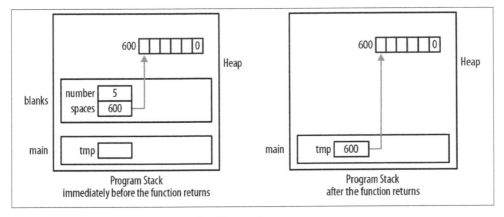

Figure 5-14. Returning dynamically allocated string

```
char *tmp = blanks(5);
printf("[%s]\n",tmp);
free(tmp);
```

Returning the address of a local string

Returning the address of a local string will be a problem since the memory will be corrupted when it is overwritten by another stack frame. This approach should be avoided; it is explained here to demonstrate the potential problems with the course of action.

We rewrite the blanks function from the previous section as shown below. Instead of dynamically allocating memory, an array is declared within the function and will subsequently be located in a stack frame. The function returns the array's address:

```
#define MAX_TAB_LENGTH 32

char* blanks(int number) {
    char spaces[MAX_TAB_LENGTH];
    int i;
    for (i = 0; i < number && i < MAX_TAB_LENGTH; i++) {
        spaces[i] = ' ';
    }
    spaces[i] = '\0';
    return spaces;
}
```

When the function executes it will return the string's address, but that memory area will subsequently be overwritten by the next function called. When this pointer is dereferenced, the contents of this memory location may have been changed. The program stack's state is illustrated in Figure 5-15.

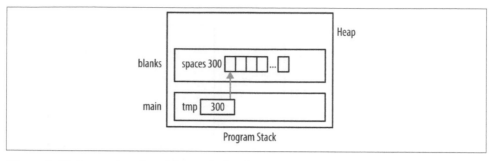

Figure 5-15. Returning the address of a local string

Function Pointers and Strings

Function pointers are discussed in depth in "Function Pointers" on page 71. They can be a flexible means of controlling how a program executes. In this section, we will demonstrate this capability by passing a comparison function to a sort function. Within a sort function, comparison of the array's elements are made to determine whether the array's elements need to be swapped. The comparison determines whether the array is sorted in ascending or descending order, or by some other sorting criteria. By passing a function to control the comparison, the function is more flexible. By passing different comparison functions, we can have the same sort function perform in different ways.

The comparison functions we will use determine the sorting order based on the case of the array's elements. The following two functions, compare and compareIgnoreCase, compare two strings based on the case of the strings. The compareIgnoreCase function converts the strings to lower case before it uses the strcmp function to compare the strings. The strcmp function was discussed in the section "Comparing Strings" on page 115. The stringToLower function returns a pointer to dynamically allocated memory. This means we need to free it when we no longer need it:

```
int compare(const char* s1, const char* s2) {
    return strcmp(s1,s2);
}

int compareIgnoreCase(const char* s1, const char* s2) {
    char* t1 = stringToLower(s1);
    char* t2 = stringToLower(s2);
    int result = strcmp(t1, t2);
    free(t1);
    free(t2);
    return result;
}
```

The stringToLower function is shown below. It returns a lowercase equivalent of the string passed to it:

```c
char* stringToLower(const char* string) {
    char *tmp = (char*) malloc(strlen(string) + 1);
    char *start = tmp;
    while (*string != 0) {
        *tmp++ = tolower(*string++);
    }
    *tmp = 0;
    return start;
}
```

The function pointer to be used is declared using a type definition as shown below:

```c
typedef int (*ftprOperation)(const char*,const char*)
```

The following sort function's implementation is based on the bubble sort algorithm. It is passed the array's address, its size, and a pointer to the function controlling the sort. In the if statement, the function passed is invoked with two elements of the array. It determines whether the array's two elements will be swapped.

```c
void sort(char *array[], int size, fptrOperation operation) {
    int swap = 1;
    while(swap) {
        swap = 0;
        for(int i=0; i<size-1; i++) {
            if(operation(array[i],array[i+1]) > 0){
                swap = 1;
                char *tmp = array[i];
                array[i] = array[i+1];
                array[i+1] = tmp;
            }
        }
    }
}
```

A display function will show the array's contents:

```c
void displayNames(char* names[], int size) {
    for(int i=0; i<size; i++) {
        printf("%s    ",names[i]);
    }
    printf("\n");
}
```

We can invoke the sort function using either of the two comparison functions. The following uses the compare function to perform a case-sensitive sort:

```c
char* names[] = {"Bob", "Ted", "Carol", "Alice", "alice"};
sort(names,5,compare);
displayNames(names,5);
```

The output of this sequence follows:

```
Alice   Bob   Carol   Ted   alice
```

If we had used the `compareIgnoreCase` function instead, then our output would appear as shown below:

```
Alice    alice    Bob    Carol    Ted
```

This makes the `sort` function much more flexible. We can now devise and pass as simple or complex an operation as we want to control the sort without having to write different `sort` functions for different sorting needs.

Summary

In this chapter, we focused on string operations and the use of pointers. The structure of strings and where they are located in memory impacts their use. Pointers provide a flexible tool for working with strings but also offer numerous opportunities to misuse strings.

String literals and the use of a literal pool were covered. Understanding literals helps explain why certain string assignment operations do not always behave as expected. This is closely related to string initialization, which was addressed in detail. Several standard string operations were examined and potential problems were identified.

Passing and returning strings to functions are common operations. The issues and potential problems with these type of operations were detailed, including the problems potentially occurring when returning a local string. The use of a pointer to a constant character was also discussed.

Finally, function pointers were used to demonstrate a powerful approach for writing sort functions. The approach is not limited to the sort operation but can be applied to other areas.

CHAPTER 6

Pointers and Structures

Structures in C can represent data structure elements, such as the nodes of a linked list or tree. Pointers provide the glue that ties these elements together. Understanding the versatility supported by pointers for common data structures will facilitate your ability to create your own data structures. In this chapter, we will explore the fundamentals of structure memory allocation in C and the implementation of several common data structures.

Structures enhance the utility of collections such as arrays. To create an array of entities such as a color type with multiple fields without using a structure, it is necessary to declare an array for each field and keep each value for a field in the same index of each array. However, with a structure, we can declare a single array where each element is an instance of the structure.

This chapter expands on the pointer concepts learned so far. This includes the introduction of pointer notation as used with structures, a discussion of how memory is allocated for a structure, a technique for managing memory used by structures, and uses of function pointers.

We will start with a discussion of how memory is allocated for a structure. An understanding of this allocation will explain how various operations work. This is followed by the introduction of a technique to minimize the overhead of heap management.

The last section illustrates how to create a number of data structures using pointers. The linked list is discussed first and will serve as the basis for several other data structures. The tree data structure is discussed last and does not use a linked list.

Introduction

A structure in C can be declared in a number of ways. In this section we will only examine two approaches, as our focus is on their use with pointers. In the first approach, we declare a structure using the `struct` keyword. In the second approach, we use a type definition. In the following declaration, the structure's name is prefixed with an underscore. This is not necessary but is often used as a naming convention. The `_person` structure includes fields for name, title, and age:

```
struct _person {
    char* firstName;
    char* lastName;
    char* title;
    unsigned int age;
};
```

A structure's declaration frequently uses the `typedef` keyword to simplify its use later in a program. The following illustrates its use with the `_person` structure:

```
typedef struct _person {
    char* firstName;
    char* lastName;
    char* title;
    unsigned int age;
} Person;
```

An instance of a person is declared as follows:

```
Person person;
```

Alternately, we can declare a pointer to a `Person` and allocate memory for it, as shown below:

```
Person *ptrPerson;
ptrPerson = (Person*) malloc(sizeof(Person));
```

If we use a simple declaration of a structure as we did with `person`, we use the dot notation to access its fields. In the following example, we assign values to the `first Name` and `age` fields:

```
Person person;
person.firstName = (char*)malloc(strlen("Emily")+1);
strcpy(person.firstName,"Emily");
person.age = 23;
```

However, if we are using a pointer to a structure, we need to use the points-to operator, as follows. This operator consists of a dash followed by the greater than symbol:

```
Person *ptrPerson;
ptrPerson = (Person*)malloc(sizeof(Person));
ptrPerson->firstName = (char*)malloc(strlen("Emily")+1);
strcpy(ptrPerson->firstName,"Emily");
ptrPerson->age = 23;
```

We do not have to use the points-to operator. Instead, we can dereference the pointer first and then apply the dot operator. This is illustrated below, where we duplicate the previous assignments:

```
Person *ptrPerson;
ptrPerson = (Person*)malloc(sizeof(Person));
(*ptrPerson).firstName = (char*)malloc(strlen("Emily")+1);
strcpy((*ptrPerson).firstName,"Emily");
(*ptrPerson).age = 23;
```

This approach is more awkward but you may see it used at times.

How Memory Is Allocated for a Structure

When a structure is allocated memory, the amount allocated to the structure is at minimum the sum of the size of its individual fields. However, the size is often larger than this sum because padding can occur between fields of a structure. This padding can result from the need to align certain data types on specific boundaries. For example, a short is typically aligned on an address evenly divisible by two while an integer is aligned on an address even divisible by four.

Several implications are related to this allocation of extra memory:

- Pointer arithmetic must be used with care
- Arrays of structures may have extra memory between their elements

For example, when an instance of the Person structure presented in the previous section is allocated memory, it will be allocated 16 bytes—4 bytes for each element. The following alternate version of Person uses a short instead of an unsigned integer for age. This will result in the same amount of memory being allocated. This is because two bytes are padded at the end of the structure:

```
typedef struct _alternatePerson {
    char* firstName;
    char* lastName;
    char* title;
    short age;
} AlternatePerson;
```

In the following sequence, we declare an instance of both a Person and an Alternate Person structure. The structures' sizes are then displayed. Their size will be the same, 16 bytes:

```
Person person;
AlternatePerson otherPerson;

printf("%d\n",sizeof(Person));            // Displays 16
printf("%d\n",sizeof(AlternatePerson));   // Displays 16
```

If we create an array of `AlternatePerson`, as shown below, there will be padding between the array's elements. This is illustrated in Figure 6-1. The shaded area shows the gaps between the array elements.

```
AlternatePerson people[30];
```

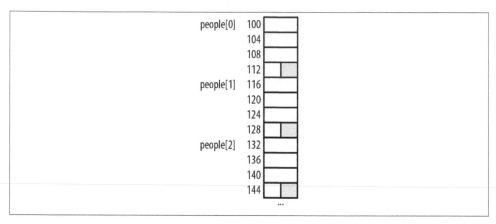

Figure 6-1. Array of AlternativePerson

If we had moved the `age` field between two fields of the structure, the gap would be internal to the structure. Depending on how the structure is accessed, this may be significant.

Structure Deallocation Issues

When memory is allocated for a structure, the runtime system will not automatically allocate memory for any pointers defined within it. Likewise, when the structure goes away, the runtime system will not automatically deallocate memory assigned to the structure's pointers.

Consider the following structure:

```
typedef struct _person {
    char* firstName;
    char* lastName;
    char* title;
    uint age;
} Person;
```

When we declare a variable of this type or dynamically allocate memory for this type, the three pointers will contain garbage. However, when a declared variable of a structure type has static storage duration (i.e., is declared outside all functions--global variable-- or is declared as static within a function), then the structure members are initialized to

0 (NULL for pointers).In the next sequence, we declare a `Person`. Its memory allocation is shown in Figure 6-2. The three dots indicate uninitialized memory:

```
void processPerson() {
   Person person;
   ...
}
```

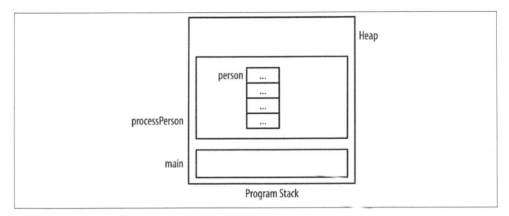

Figure 6-2. Person structure uninitialized

During the initialization of this structure, each field will be assigned a value. The pointer fields will be allocated from the heap and assigned to each pointer:

```
void initializePerson(Person *person, const char* fn,
      const char* ln, const char* title, uint age) {
   person->firstName = (char*) malloc(strlen(fn) + 1);
   strcpy(person->firstName, fn);
   person->lastName = (char*) malloc(strlen(ln) + 1);
   strcpy(person->lastName, ln);
   person->title = (char*) malloc(strlen(title) + 1);
   strcpy(person->title, title);
   person->age = age;
}
```

We can use this function as shown below. Figure 6-3 illustrates how memory is allocated:

```
void processPerson() {
   Person person;
   initializePerson(&person, "Peter", "Underwood", "Manager", 36);
   ...
}
int main() {
   processPerson();
   ...
}
```

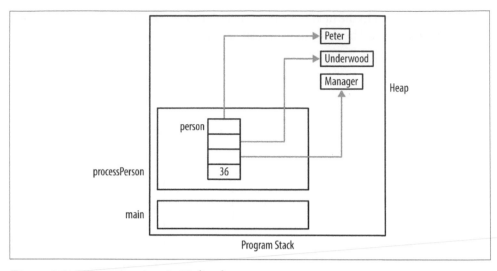

Figure 6-3. Person structure initialized

Since this declaration was part of a function, when the function returns the memory for
person will go away. However, the dynamically allocated strings were not released and
are still in the heap. Unfortunately, we have lost their address and we cannot free them,
resulting in a memory leak.

When we are through with the instance, we need to deallocate the memory. The following function will free up the memory we previously allocated when we created the
instance:

```
void deallocatePerson(Person *person) {
    free(person->firstName);
    free(person->lastName);
    free(person->title);
}
```

This function needs to be invoked before the function terminates:

```
void processPerson() {
    Person person;
    initializePerson(&person, "Peter", "Underwood", "Manager", 36);
    ...
    deallocatePerson(&person);
}
```

Unfortunately, we must remember to call the initialize and deallocate functions.
The automatic invocation of these operations against an object is performed in object-
oriented programming languages such as C++.

If we use a pointer to a Person, we need to remember to free up the person as shown
below:

```
void processPerson() {
    Person *ptrPerson;
    ptrPerson = (Person*) malloc(sizeof(Person));
    initializePerson(ptrPerson, "Peter", "Underwood", "Manager", 36);
        ...
    deallocatePerson(ptrPerson);
    free(ptrPerson);
}
```

Figure 6-4 illustrates how memory is allocated.

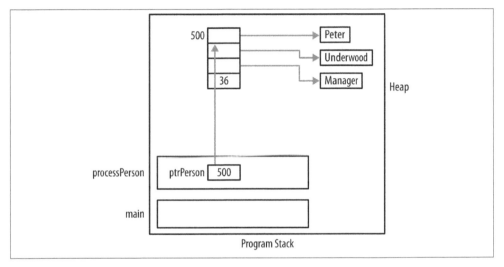

Figure 6-4. Pointer to a person instance

Avoiding malloc/free Overhead

When structures are allocated and then deallocated repeatedly, some overhead will be incurred, resulting in a potentially significant performance penalty. One approach to deal with this problem is to maintain your own list of allocated structures. When a user no longer needs an instance of a structure, it is returned to the pool. When an instance is needed, it obtains the object from the pool. If there are no elements available in the pool, a new instance is dynamically allocated. This approach effectively maintains a pool of structures that can be used and reused as needed.

To demonstrate this approach we will use the Person structure previously defined. A pool of persons is maintained in an array. A more complex list, such as a linked list, can also be used, as illustrated in the section "Single-Linked List" on page 142. To keep this example simple, an array of pointers is used, as declared below:

```
#define LIST_SIZE 10
Person *list[LIST_SIZE];
```

Before the list can be used, it needs to be initialized. The following function assigns NULL to each element of the array:

```
void initializeList() {
    for(int i=0; i<LIST_SIZE; i++) {
        list[i] = NULL;
    }
}
```

Two functions are used to add and retrieve persons. The first is the getPerson function, as shown below. This function retrieves a person from the list if possible. The array's elements are compared to NULL. The first non-null element is returned, and its position in list is then assigned a value of NULL. If there is no person available, then a new instance of a Person is created and returned. This avoids the overhead of dynamically allocating memory for a person every time a new one is needed. We only allocate memory if there is none in the pool. The initialization of the instance returned can be done either before it is returned or by the caller, depending on the needs of the application:

```
Person *getPerson() {
    for(int i=0; i<LIST_SIZE; i++) {
        if(list[i] != NULL) {
            Person *ptr = list[i];
            list[i] = NULL;
            return ptr;
        }
    }
    Person *person = (Person*)malloc(sizeof(Person));
    return person;
}
```

The second function is the returnPerson, which either adds the person to the list or frees it up. The array's elements are checked to see whether there are any NULL values. If it does, then person is added to that position and the pointer is returned. If the list is full, then the pointers within person are freed using the deallocatePerson function, person is freed, and then NULL is returned:

```
Person *returnPerson(Person *person) {
    for(int i=0; i<LIST_SIZE; i++) {
        if(list[i] == NULL) {
            list[i] = person;
            return person;
        }
    }
    deallocatePerson(person);
    free(person);
    return NULL;
}
```

The following illustrates the initialization of the list and adding a person to the list:

```
initializeList();
Person *ptrPerson;

ptrPerson = getPerson();
initializePerson(ptrPerson,"Ralph","Fitsgerald","Mr.",35);
displayPerson(*ptrPerson);
returnPerson(ptrPerson);
```

One problem associated with this approach deals with the list size. If the list is too small, then more dynamic allocation and deallocation of memory will be necessary. If the list is large and the structures are not being used, a potentially large amount of memory may be tied up and unavailable for other uses. A more sophisticated list management scheme can be used to manage the list's size.

Using Pointers to Support Data Structures

Pointers can provide more flexible support for simple and complex data structures. The flexibility can be attributed to the dynamic allocation of memory and the ease of changing pointer references. The memory does not have to be contiguous, as is the case with arrays. Only the exact amount of memory needs to be allocated.

In this section, we will examine how several commonly used data structures can be implemented using pointers. Numerous C libraries provide equivalent and more extensive support than those illustrated here. However, understanding how they can be implemented can prove to be useful when implementing nonstandard data structures. On some platforms, the libraries may not be available, and the developer will need to implement their own version.

We will examine four different data structures:

Linked list
    A single-linked list

Queue
    A simple first-in first-out queue

Stack
    A simple stack

Tree
    A binary tree

Along with these data structures, we will incorporate function pointers to illustrate their power in dealing with generic structures. The linked list is a very useful data structure, and we will use it as the foundation of the queue's and stack's implementation.

We will illustrate each of these data structures using an employee structure. For example, a linked list consists of nodes connected to one another. Each node will hold user-supplied data. The simple employee structure is listed below. The `unsigned char` data type is used for age, as this will be large enough to hold people's ages:

```
typedef struct _employee{
    char name[32];
    unsigned char age;
} Employee;
```

A simple array is used for a single name. While a pointer to `char` may prove to be a more flexible data type for this field, we have elected to use an array of `char` to simplify the examples.

Two comparison functions will be developed. The first one compares two employees and returns an integer. This function is modeled after the `strcmp` function. A return value of 0 means the two employee structures are considered to be equal to each other. A return value of –1 means the first employee precedes the second employee alphabetically. A return value of 1 means the first employee follows the second employee. The second function displays a single employee:

```
int compareEmployee(Employee *e1, Employee *e2) {
    return strcmp(e1->name, e2->name);
}

void displayEmployee(Employee* employee) {
    printf("%s\t%d\n", employee->name, employee->age);
}
```

In addition, two function pointers will be used as defined below. The `DISPLAY` function pointer designates a function that is passed a pointer to void and returns void. Its intent is to display data. The second pointer, `COMPARE`, represents a function used to compare data referenced by two pointers. The function should compare the data and return either a 0, –1, or 1, as explained with the `compareEmployee` function:

```
typedef void(*DISPLAY)(void*);
typedef int(*COMPARE)(void*, void*);
```

Single-Linked List

A linked list is a data structure that consists of a series of nodes interconnected with links. Typically, one node is called the head node and subsequent nodes follow the head, one after another. The last node is called the *tail*. The links connecting the nodes are easily implemented using a pointer. Each node can be dynamically allocated as needed.

This approach is preferable to an array of nodes. Using an array results in the creation of a fixed number of nodes regardless of how many nodes may be needed. Links are implemented using the index of the array's elements. Using an array is not as flexible as using dynamic memory allocation and pointers.

For example, if we wanted to change the order of elements of the array, it would be necessary to copy both elements, and that can be large for a structure. In addition, adding or removing an element may require moving large portions of the array to make room for the new element or to remove an existing element.

There are several types of linked lists. The simplest is a single-linked list where there is a single link from one node to the next. The links start at the head and eventually leads to the tail. A circular-linked list has no tail. The linked list's last node points back to the head. A doubly linked list uses two links, one pointing forward and one pointing backward so that you can navigate through the list in both directions. This type of linked list is more flexible but is more difficult to implement. Figure 6-5 conceptually illustrates these types of linked lists.

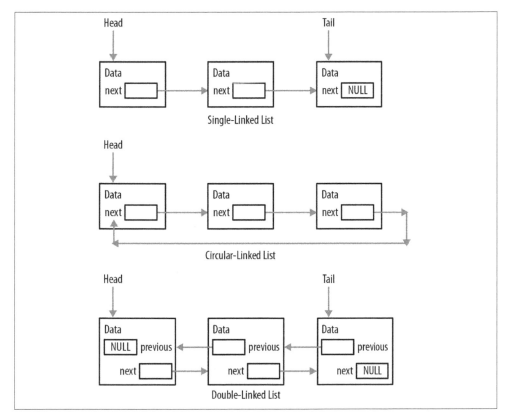

Figure 6-5. Linked list types

In this section, we will illustrate the construction and use of a single-linked list. The following shows the structure used to support the linked list. A Node structure is defined to represent a node. It consists of two pointers. The first one, a pointer to void, holds an arbitrary data type. The second is a pointer to the next node. The LinkedList structure represents the linked list and holds a pointer to the head and the tail. The current pointer will help traverse the linked list:

```
typedef struct _node {
    void *data;
    struct _node *next;
} Node;

typedef struct _linkedList {
    Node *head;
    Node *tail;
    Node *current;
} LinkedList;
```

We will develop several functions that use these structures to support linked list functionality:

void initializeList(LinkedList*)	Initializes the linked list
void addHead(LinkedList*, void*)	Adds data to the linked list's head
void addTail(LinkedList*, void*)	Adds data to the linked list's tail
void delete(LinkedList*, Node*)	Removes a node from the linked list
Node *getNode(LinkedList*, COMPARE, void*)	Returns a pointer to the node containing a specific data item
void displayLinkedList(LinkedList*, DISPLAY)	Displays the linked list

Before the linked list can be used it needs to be initialized. The initializeList function, shown below, performs this task. A pointer to the LinkedList object is passed to the function where each pointer in the structure is set to NULL:

```
void initializeList(LinkedList *list) {
    list->head = NULL;
    list->tail = NULL;
    list->current = NULL;
}
```

The addHead and addTail functions add data to the linked list's head and tail, respectively. In this linked list implementation, the add and delete functions are responsible for allocating and freeing memory used by the linked list's nodes. This removes this responsibility from the user of the linked list.

In the addHead function listed below, memory is first allocated for the node and the data passed to the function is assigned to the structure's data field. By passing the data as a pointer to void, the linked list is able to hold any type of data the user wants to use.

Next, we check to see whether the linked list is empty. If so, we assign the tail pointer to the node and assign NULL to the node's next field. If not, the node's next pointer is assigned to the list's head. Regardless, the list's head is assigned to the node:

```
void addHead(LinkedList *list, void* data) {
    Node *node = (Node*) malloc(sizeof(Node));
    node->data = data;
    if (list->head == NULL) {
        list->tail = node;
        node->next = NULL;
    } else {
        node->next = list->head;
    }
    list->head = node;
}
```

The following code sequence illustrates using the initializeList and addHead functions. Three employees are added to the list. Figure 6-6 shows how memory is allocated after these statements execute. Some arrows have been removed to simplify the diagram. In addition, the Employee structure's name array has been simplified:

```
LinkedList linkedList;

Employee *samuel = (Employee*) malloc(sizeof(Employee));
strcpy(samuel->name, "Samuel");
samuel->age = 32;

Employee *sally = (Employee*) malloc(sizeof(Employee));
strcpy(sally->name, "Sally");
sally->age = 28;

Employee *susan = (Employee*) malloc(sizeof(Employee));
strcpy(susan->name, "Susan");
susan->age = 45;

initializeList(&linkedList);

addHead(&linkedList, samuel);
addHead(&linkedList, sally);
addHead(&linkedList, susan);
```

The addTail function is shown below. It starts by allocating memory for a new node and assigning the data to the data field. Since the node will always be added to the tail, the node's next field is assigned to NULL. If the linked list is empty, then the head pointer will be NULL and head can be assigned to the new node. If it is not NULL, then the tail's next pointer is assigned to the new node. Regardless, the linked list's tail pointer is assigned to the node:

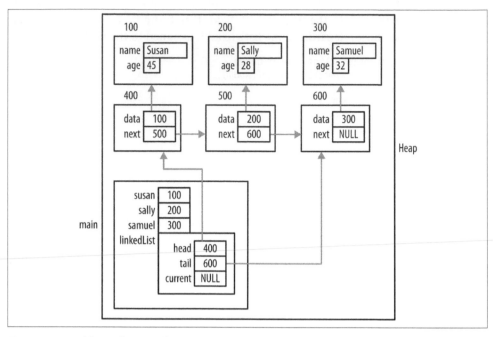

Figure 6-6. addHead example

```
void addTail(LinkedList *list, void* data) {
    Node *node = (Node*) malloc(sizeof(Node));
    node->data = data;
    node->next = NULL;
    if (list->head == NULL) {
        list->head = node;
    } else {
        list->tail->next = node;
    }
    list->tail = node;
}
```

In the following sequence, the addTail function is illustrated. The creation of the employee objects has not been duplicated here. The employees have been added in the opposite order from the previous example using the addTail function. This results in the memory allocation being the same as shown in Figure 6-6:

```
initializeList(&linkedList);

addTail(&linkedList, susan);
addTail(&linkedList, sally);
addTail(&linkedList, samuel);
```

The delete function will remove a node from the linked list. To simplify this function, a pointer to the node to be deleted is passed to it. The function's user probably has a pointer to the data but not to the node holding the data. To aid in identifying the node, a helper function has been provided to return a pointer to the node: getNode. The getNode function is passed three parameters:

- A pointer to the linked list
- A pointer to a comparison function
- A pointer to the data to be found

The code for the getNode function follows. The variable node initially points to the list's head and traverses the list until either a match is found or the linked list's end is encountered. The compare function is invoked to determine whether a match is found. When the two data items are equal, it returns a zero.

```
Node *getNode(LinkedList *list, COMPARE compare , void* data) {
    Node *node = list->head;
    while (node != NULL) {
        if (compare(node->data, data) == 0) {
            return node;
        }
        node = node->next;
    }
    return NULL;
}
```

The compare function illustrates using a function pointer at runtime to determine which function to use to perform a comparison. This adds considerable flexibility to the linked list implementation because we do not need to hard code the comparison function's name in the getNode function.

The delete function follows. To keep the function simple, it does not always check for null values in the linked list or the node passed. The first if statement handles a node to be deleted from the head. If the head node is the only node, then the head and tail are assigned null values. Otherwise, the head is assigned to the node following the head.

The else statement traverses the list from head to tail using a tmp pointer. The while loop will terminate if either tmp is assigned NULL, indicating the node does not exist in the list, or the node following tmp is the node we are looking for. Since this is a single-linked list, we need to know which node precedes the target node to be deleted. This knowledge is needed to assign the node following the target node to the preceding node's next field. At the end of the delete function, the node is freed. The user is responsible for deleting the data pointed to by this node before the delete function is called.

```
void delete(LinkedList *list, Node *node) {
    if (node == list->head) {
        if (list->head->next == NULL) {
            list->head = list->tail = NULL;
        } else {
```

```
            list->head = list->head->next;
        }
    } else {
        Node *tmp = list->head;
        while (tmp != NULL && tmp->next != node) {
            tmp = tmp->next;
        }
        if (tmp != NULL) {
            tmp->next = node->next;
        }
    }
    free(node);
}
```

The next sequence demonstrates the use of this function. The three employees are added to the linked list's head. We will use the compareEmployee function as described in the section "Using Pointers to Support Data Structures" on page 141 to perform comparisons:

```
addHead(&linkedList, samuel);
addHead(&linkedList, sally);
addHead(&linkedList, susan);

Node *node = getNode(&linkedList,
        (int (*)(void*, void*))compareEmployee, sally);
delete(&linkedList, node);
```

When this sequence executes, the program stack and heap will appear as illustrated in Figure 6-7.

The displayLinkedList function illustrates how to traverse a linked list as shown below. It starts at the head and displays each element using the function passed as the second argument. The node pointer is assigned the next field's value and will terminate when the last node is displayed:

```
void displayLinkedList(LinkedList *list, DISPLAY display) {
    printf("\nLinked List\n");
    Node *current = list->head;
    while (current != NULL) {
        display(current->data);
        current = current->next;
    }
}
```

The following illustrates this function using the displayEmployee function developed in the section "Using Pointers to Support Data Structures" on page 141:

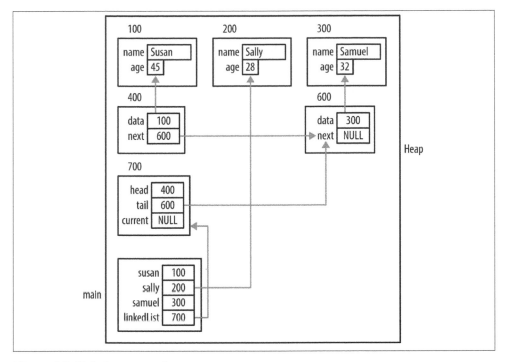

Figure 6-7. Deletion example

```
addHead(&linkedList, samuel);
addHead(&linkedList, sally);
addHead(&linkedList, susan);

displayLinkedList(&linkedList, (DISPLAY)displayEmployee);
```

The output of this sequence follows:

```
Linked List
Susan     45
Sally     28
Samuel    32
```

Using Pointers to Support a Queue

A queue is a linear data structure whose behavior is similar to a waiting line. It typically supports two primary operations: enqueue and dequeue. The enqueue operation adds an element to the queue. The dequeue operation removes an element from the queue. Normally, the first element added to a queue is the first element dequeued from a queue. This behavior is referred to as First-In-First-Out (FIFO).

A linked list is frequently used to implement a queue. The enqueue operation will add a node to the linked list's head and the dequeue operation will remove a node from the tail. To illustrate the queue, we will use the linked list developed in the "Single-Linked List" on page 142.

Let's start by using a type definition statement to define a term for queue. It will be based on a linked list as shown below. We can now use Queue to clearly designate our intent:

```
typedef LinkedList Queue;
```

To implement the initialization operation, all we need to do is use the function initializeList. Instead of calling this function directly, we will use the following initializeQueue function:

```
void initializeQueue(Queue *queue) {
    initializeList(queue);
}
```

In a similar manner, the following will add a node to a queue using the addHead function:

```
void enqueue(Queue *queue, void *node) {
    addHead(queue, node);
}
```

The previous linked list implementation does not have an explicit function to remove the tail node. The dequeue function that follows removes the last node. Three conditions are handled:

An empty queue
    NULL is returned

A single node queue
    Handled by the else if statement

A multiple node queue
    Handled by the else clause

In the latter case, the tmp pointer is advanced node by node until it points to the node immediately preceding the tail node. Three operations are then performed in the following sequence:

1. The tail is assigned to the tmp node

2. The tmp pointer is advanced to the next node

3. The tail's next field is set to NULL to indicate there are no more nodes in the queue

This order is necessary to ensure the list's integrity, as illustrated conceptually in Figure 6-8. The circled numbers correspond to the three steps listed above:

```
void *dequeue(Queue *queue) {
    Node *tmp = queue->head;
    void *data;
```

```
    if (queue->head == NULL) {
        data = NULL;
    } else if (queue->head == queue->tail) {
        queue->head = queue->tail = NULL;
        data = tmp->data;
        free(tmp);
    } else {
        while (tmp->next != queue->tail) {
            tmp = tmp->next;
        }
        queue->tail = tmp;
        tmp = tmp->next;
        queue->tail->next = NULL;
        data = tmp->data;
        free(tmp);
    }
    return data;
}
```

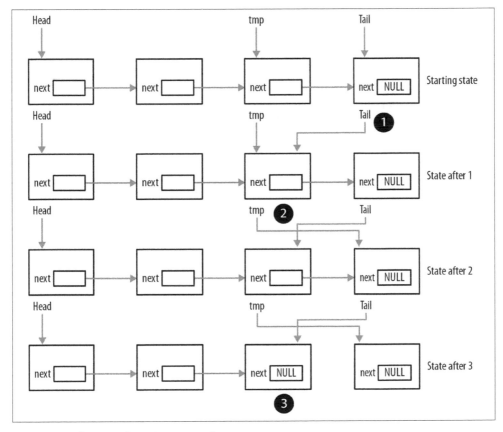

Figure 6-8. dequeue function example

The data assigned to the node is returned, and the node is freed. These functions are illustrated in the following code sequence using the employees created earlier:

```
Queue queue;
initializeQueue(&queue);

enqueue(&queue, samuel);
enqueue(&queue, sally);
enqueue(&queue, susan);

void *data = dequeue(&queue);
printf("Dequeued %s\n", ((Employee*) data)->name);
data = dequeue(&queue);
printf("Dequeued %s\n", ((Employee*) data)->name);
data = dequeue(&queue);
printf("Dequeued %s\n", ((Employee*) data)->name);
```

The output of this sequence follows:

```
Dequeued Samuel
Dequeued Sally
Dequeued Susan
```

Using Pointers to Support a Stack

The stack data structure is also a type of list. In this case, elements are pushed onto the stack's top and then popped off. When multiple elements are pushed and then popped, the stack exhibits First-In-Last-Out (FILO) behavior. The first element pushed on to the stack is the last element popped off.

Like the queue's implementation, we can use a linked list to support stack operations. The two most common operations are the push and pop operations. The push operation is effected using the addHead function. The pop operation requires adding a new function to remove the head node. We start by defining a stack in terms of a linked list as follows:

```
typedef LinkedList Stack;
```

To initialize the stack, we add an initializeStack function. This function calls the initializeList function:

```
void initializeStack(Stack *stack) {
    initializeList(stack);
}
```

The push operation calls the addHead function as shown below:

```
void push(Stack *stack, void* data) {
    addHead(stack, data);
}
```

The pop operation's implementation follows. We start by assigning the stack's head to a node pointer. It involves handling three conditions:

The stack is empty
> The function returns NULL

The stack contains a single element
> If the node points to the tail then the head and tail are the same element. The head and tail are assigned NULL, and the data is returned.

The stack contains more than one element
> In this case, the head is assigned to the next element in the list, and the data is returned.

In the latter two cases, the node is freed:

```
void *pop(Stack *stack) {
    Node *node = stack->head;
    if (node == NULL) {
        return NULL;
    } else if (node == stack->tail) {
        stack->head = stack->tail = NULL;
        void *data = node->data;
        free(node);
        return data;
    } else {
        stack->head = stack->head->next;
        void *data = node->data;
        free(node);
        return data;
    }
}
```

We will reuse the employees' instances created in the section "Single-Linked List" on page 142 to demonstrate the stack. The following code sequence will push three employees and then pop them off the stack:

```
Stack stack;
initializeStack(&stack);

push(&stack, samuel);
push(&stack, sally);
push(&stack, susan);

Employee *employee;

for(int i=0; i<4; i++) {
    employee = (Employee*) pop(&stack);
    printf("Popped %s\n", employee->name);
}
```

When executed, we get the following output. Because we used the pop function four times, NULL was returned the last time:

```
Popped Susan
Popped Sally
Popped Samuel
Popped (null)
```

Other stack operations sometime include a peek operation where the top element is returned but is not popped off the stack.

Using Pointers to Support a Tree

The tree is a very useful data structure whose name is derived from the relationship between its elements. Typically, child nodes are attached to a parent node. The overall form is an inverted tree where a root node represents the data structure's starting element.

A tree can have any number of children nodes. However, binary trees are more common where each node possesses zero, one, or two children nodes. The children are designated as either the left child or the right child. Nodes with no children are called leaf nodes, similar to the leaves of a tree. The examples presented in this section will illustrate a binary tree.

Pointers provide an obvious and dynamic way of maintaining the relationship between tree nodes. Nodes can be dynamically allocated and added to a tree as needed. We will use the following structure for a node. Using a pointer to void allows us to handle any type of data that we need:

```
typedef struct _tree {
    void *data;
    struct _tree *left;
    struct _tree *right;
} TreeNode;
```

When we add nodes to a tree, it makes sense to add them in a particular order. This will make many operations, such as searching, easier. A common ordering is to add a new node to a tree such that all of the node's children on the left possess a value less than the parent node and all of the children on the right possess a value greater than the parent node. This is called a binary search tree.

The following insertNode function will insert a node into a binary search tree. However, to insert a node, a comparison needs to be performed between the new node and the tree's existing nodes. We use the COMPARE function pointer to pass the comparison function's address. The first part of the function allocates memory for a new node and assigns the data to the node. The left and right children are set to NULL since new nodes are always added as leaves to a tree:

```
void insertNode(TreeNode **realRoot, COMPARE compare, void* data) {
    TreeNode *node = (TreeNode*) malloc(sizeof (TreeNode));
    node->data = data;
    node->left = NULL;
    node->right = NULL;

    TreeNode *root = *realRoot;

    if (root == NULL) {
        *realRoot = node;
        return;
    }

    while (1) {
        if (compare((root)->data, data) > 0) {
            if ((root)->left != NULL) {
                root = (root)->left;
            } else {
                (root)->left = node;
                break;
            }
        } else {
            if ((root)->right != NULL) {
                root = (root)->right;
            } else {
                (root)->right = node;
                break;
            }
        }
    }
}
```

First, the root is checked to determine whether the tree is empty. If it is, then a new node is assigned to the root and the function returns. The root is passed as a pointer to a pointer to a TreeNode. This is necessary because we want to modify the pointer passed to the function, not what the pointer points to. This use of two levels of indirection is detailed in "Multiple Levels of Indirection" on page 25.

If the tree is not empty, then an infinite loop is entered and will terminate when the new node has been added to the tree. With each loop's iteration, the new node and current parent node are compared. On the basis of this comparison, the local root pointer will be reassigned to either the left or right child. This root pointer points to the current node in the tree. If the left or right child is NULL, then the node is added as a child and the loop terminates.

To demonstrate insertNode function, we will reuse the employee instances created in the section "Using Pointers to Support Data Structures" on page 141. The following sequence initializes an empty TreeNode and then inserts the three employees. The resulting program stack's and heap's state is illustrated in Figure 6-9. Some lines pointing to the employees have been removed to simplify the diagram. The nodes' placement in the heap have also been arranged to reflect the tree structure's order:

```
TreeNode *tree = NULL;

insertNode(&tree, (COMPARE) compareEmployee, samuel);
insertNode(&tree, (COMPARE) compareEmployee, sally);
insertNode(&tree, (COMPARE) compareEmployee, susan);
```

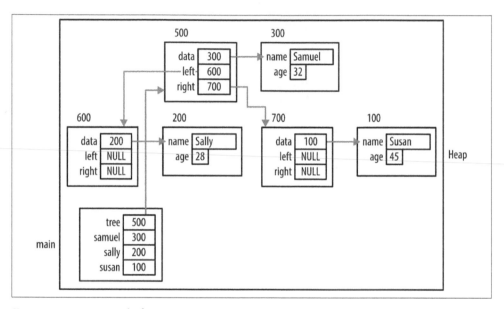

Figure 6-9. insertNode function

Figure 6-10 illustrates the logical structure of this tree.

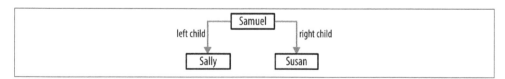

Figure 6-10. Logical tree organization

Binary trees are used for a number of purposes and can be traversed in three different ways: pre-order, in-order, and post-order. The three techniques use the same steps, but they are performed in different orders. The three steps are:

Visit the node
    Process the node

Go left
> Transfer to the left node

Go right
> Transfer to the right node

For our purposes, visiting a node means we will display its contents. The three orders are:

In-order
> Go left, visit the node, go right

Pre-order
> Visit the node, go left, go right

Post-order
> Go left, go right, visit the node

The functions' implementations are shown below. Each passes the tree's root and a function pointer for the display function. They are recursive and will call themselves as long as the root node passed to it is not null. They only differ in the order the three steps are executed:

```
void inOrder(TreeNode *root, DISPLAY display) {
    if (root != NULL) {
        inOrder(root->left, display);
        display(root->data);
        inOrder(root->right, display);
    }
}

void postOrder(TreeNode *root, DISPLAY display) {
    if (root != NULL) {
        postOrder(root->left, display);
        postOrder(root->right, display);
        display(root->data);
    }
}

void preOrder(TreeNode *root, DISPLAY display) {
    if (root != NULL) {
        display(root->data);
        preOrder(root->left, display);
        preOrder(root->right, display);
    }
}
```

The following code sequence invokes these functions:

```
preOrder(tree, (DISPLAY) displayEmployee);
inOrder(tree, (DISPLAY) displayEmployee);
postOrder(tree, (DISPLAY) displayEmployee);
```

Table 6-1 shows the output of each function call based on the previous initialization of the tree.

Table 6-1. Traversal techniques

pre-order	Samuel 32 Sally 28 Susan 45
in-order	Sally 28 Samuel 32 Susan 45
post-order	Sally 28 Susan 45 Samuel 32

The in-order traversal will return a sorted list of the tree's members. The pre-order and post-order traversal can be used to evaluate arithmetic expressions when used in conjunction with a stack and queue.

Summary

The power and flexibility of pointers is exemplified when used to create and support data structures. Combined with dynamic memory allocation of structures, pointers enable the creation of data structures that use memory efficiently and can grow and shrink to meet the application's needs.

We started this chapter with a discussion of how memory is allocated for structures. Padding between the field's structures and between arrays of structures is possible. Dynamic memory allocation and deallocation can be expensive. We examined one technique to maintain a pool of structures to minimize this overhead.

We also demonstrated the implementation of several commonly used data structures. The linked list was used to support several of these data structures. Function pointers were used to add flexibility to these implementations by allowing the comparison or display function to be determined at runtime.

CHAPTER 7

Security Issues and the Improper Use of Pointers

Few applications exist where security and reliability are not significant concerns. This concern is reinforced by frequent reports of security breaches and application failures. The responsibility of securing an application largely falls on the developer. In this chapter, we will examine practices to make applications more secure and reliable.

Writing secure applications in C can be difficult because of several inherent aspects of the language. For example, C does not prevent the programmer from writing outside an array's bounds. This can result in corrupted memory and introduce potential security risks. In addition, the improper use of pointers is often at the root of many security problems.

When an application behaves in unpredictable ways, it may not seem to be a security issue, at least in terms of unauthorized access. However, it is sometimes possible to take advantage of this behavior, which can result in a denial of service and thus compromise the application. Unpredictable behavior that results from improper use of pointers has been illustrated elsewhere in this book. In this chapter, we will identify additional improper usages of pointers.

The CERT (*http://www.cert.org/*) organization is a good source for a more comprehensive treatment of security issues in C and other languages. This organization studies Internet security vulnerabilities. We will focus on those security issues related to the use of pointers. Many of the CERT organization's security concerns can be traced back to the improper use of pointers. Understanding pointers and the proper ways to use them is an important tool for developing secure and reliable applications. Some of these topics have been addressed in earlier chapters, not necessarily from a security standpoint but rather from a programming practice standpoint.

There have been improvements in security introduced by operating systems (OS). Some of these improvements are reflected in how memory is used. Although improvements are typically beyond the control of developers, they will affect the program. Understanding these issues will help explain an application's behavior. We will focus on *Address Space Layout Randomization* and *Data Execution Prevention*.

The *Address Space Layout Randomization* (ASLR) process arranges an application's data region randomly in memory. These data regions include the code, stack, and heap. Randomizing the placement of these regions makes it more difficult for attackers to predict where memory will be placed and thus more difficult to use them. Certain types of attacks, such as the *return-to-libc* attack, overwrite portions of the stack and transfer control to this region. This area is frequently the shared C library, libc. If the location of the stack and libc are not known, then such attacks will be less likely to succeed.

The *Data Execution Prevention* (DEP) technique prevents the execution of code if it is in a nonexecutable region of memory. In some types of attacks, a region of memory is overwritten with a malicious code and then control is transferred to it. If this region of code is nonexecutable, such as the stack or heap, then it is prevented from executing. This technique can be implemented either in hardware or in software.

In this chapter, we will examine security issues from several perspectives:

- Declaration and initialization of pointers
- Improper pointer usage
- Deallocation problems

Pointer Declaration and Initialization

Problems can arise with the declaration and initialization of pointers or, more correctly, the failure to initialize pointers. In this section, we will examine situations where these types of problems can occur.

Improper Pointer Declaration

Consider the following declaration:

```
int* ptr1, ptr2;
```

There is nothing necessarily wrong with the declaration; however, it may not be what was intended. This declaration declared ptr1 as a pointer to an integer and ptr2 as an integer. The asterisk was purposely placed next to the data type, and a space was placed before ptr1. This placement makes no difference to the compiler, but to the reader, it may imply that both ptr1 and ptr2 are declared as pointers to integers. However, only ptr1 is a pointer.

The correct approach is to declare them both as pointers using a single line, as shown below:

```
int *ptr1, *ptr2;
```

 It is an even better practice to declare each variable on its own line.

Another good practice involves using type definitions instead of macro definitions. These definitions allow the compiler to check scoping rules, which is not always true with macro definitions.

Variables may be declared with the assistance of a directive, as shown below. Here, a pointer to an integer is wrapped in a `define` directive and then used to declare variables:

```
#define PINT int*
PINT ptr1, ptr2;
```

However, the result is the same problem as described above. A better approach is shown below using a type definition:

```
typedef int* PINT;
PINT ptr1, ptr2;
```

Both variables are declared as pointers to integers.

Failure to Initialize a Pointer Before It Is Used

Using a pointer before it is initialized can result in a run-time error. This is sometimes referred to as a *wild pointer*. A simple example follows where a pointer to an integer is declared but is never assigned a value before it is used:

```
int *pi;
...
printf("%d\n",*pi);
```

Figure 7-1 illustrates how memory is allocated at this point.

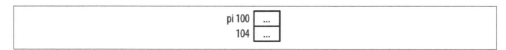

Figure 7-1. Wild pointer

The variable `pi` has not been initialized and will contain garbage, indicated by the ellipses. Most likely this sequence will terminate during execution if the memory address stored in `pi` is outside the valid address space for the application. Otherwise, the value displayed will be whatever happens to be at that address and will be presented as an integer. If we use a pointer to a string instead, we will frequently see a series of strange characters displayed until the terminating zero is reached.

Dealing with Uninitialized Pointers

Nothing inherent in a pointer tells us whether it is valid. Thus, we cannot simply examine its contents to determine whether it is valid. However, three approaches are used to deal with uninitialized pointers:

- Always initialize a pointer with NULL
- Use the assert function
- Use third-party tools

Initializing a pointer to NULL will make it easier to check for proper usage. Even then, checking for a null value can be tedious, as shown below:

```
int *pi = NULL;
...
if(pi == NULL) {
    // pi should not be dereferenced
} else {
    // pi can be used
}
```

The assert function can also be used to test for null pointer values. In the following example, the pi variable is tested for a null value. If the expression is true, then nothing happens. If the expression is false, then the program terminates. Thus, the program will terminate if the pointer is null.

```
assert(pi != NULL);
```

For debug versions of the application, this approach may be acceptable. If the pointer is null, then the output will appear similar to the following:

```
Assertion failed: pi != NULL
```

The assert function is found in the *assert.h* header file.

Third-party tools can also be used to help identify these types of problems. In addition, certain compiler options can be useful, as addressed in the section "Using Static Analysis Tools" on page 173.

Pointer Usage Issues

In this section, we will examine misuse of the dereference operator and array subscripts. We will also examine problems related to strings, structures, and function pointers.

Many security issues revolve around the concept of a buffer overflow. Buffer overflow occurs when memory outside the object's bounds is overwritten. This memory may be part of the program's address space or another process. When the memory is outside of the program address space, most operating systems will issue a segmentation fault and terminate the program. Termination for this reason constitutes a denial of service attack when done maliciously. This type of attack does not attempt to gain unauthorized access but tries to take down the application and potentially a server.

If the buffer overflow occurs within the application's address space, then it can result in unauthorized access to data and/or the transfer of control to another segment of code, thereby potentially compromising the system. This is of particular concern if the application is executing with supervisor privileges.

Buffer overflow can happen by:

- Not checking the index values used when accessing an array's elements
- Not being careful when performing pointer arithmetic with array pointers
- Using functions such as `gets` to read in a string from standard input
- Using functions such as `strcpy` and `strcat` improperly

When buffer overflow occurs with a stack frame element, it is possible to overwrite the return address portion of the stack frame with a call to malicious code created at the same time. See "Program Stack and Heap" on page 58 for more detail about the stack frame. When the function returns, it will transfer control to the malicious function. This function can then perform any operation, restrained only by the current user's privilege level.

Test for NULL

Always check the return value when using a `malloc` type function. Failure to do so can result in abnormal termination of the program. The following illustrates the general approach:

```
float *vector = malloc(20 * sizeof(float));
if(vector == NULL) {
    // malloc failed to allocate memory
} else {
    // Process vector
}
```

Misuse of the Dereference Operator

A common approach for declaring and initializing a pointer is shown below:

```
int num;
int *pi = &num;
```

Another seemingly equivalent declaration sequence follows:

```
int num;
int *pi;
*pi = &num;
```

However, this is not correct. Notice the use of the dereference operator on the last line. We are attempting to assign the address of num not to pi but rather to the memory location specified by the contents of pi. The pointer, pi, has not been initialized yet. We have made a simple mistake of misusing the dereference operator. The correct sequence follows:

```
int num;
int *pi;
pi = &num;
```

In the original declaration, int *pi = &num, the asterisk declared the variable to be a pointer. It was not used as the dereference operator.

Dangling Pointers

A dangling pointer occurs when a pointer is freed but still references that memory. This problem is described in detail in "Dangling Pointers" on page 51. If an attempt is made to access this memory later, then its contents may well have changed. A write operation against this memory may corrupt memory, and a read operation may return invalid data. Either could potentially result in the termination of the program.

This has not been considered a security concern until recently. As explained in Dangling Pointer (*http://bit.ly/14eHYOY*), there exists a potential for exploiting a dangling pointer. However, this approach is based on the exploitation of the *VTable* (Virtual Table) in C++. A VTable is an array of function pointers used to support virtual methods in C++. Unless you are using a similar approach involving function pointers, this should not be a concern in C.

Accessing Memory Outside the Bounds of an Array

Nothing can prevent a program from accessing memory outside of the space allocated for an array. In this example, we declare and initialize three arrays to demonstrate this behavior. The arrays are assumed to be allocated in consecutive memory locations.

```
char firstName[8] = "1234567";
char middleName[8] = "1234567";
char lastName[8] = "1234567";

middleName[-2] = 'X';
middleName[0] = 'X';
middleName[10] = 'X';

printf("%p  %s\n",firstName,firstName);
```

```
printf("%p  %s\n",middleName,middleName);
printf("%p  %s\n",lastName,lastName);
```

To illustrate how memory is overwritten, three arrays are initialized to a simple sequence of numbers. While the behavior of the program will vary by compiler and machine, this will normally execute and overwrite characters in firstName and lastName. The output is shown below. Figure 7-2 illustrates how memory is allocated:

```
116   12X4567
108   X234567
100   123456X
```

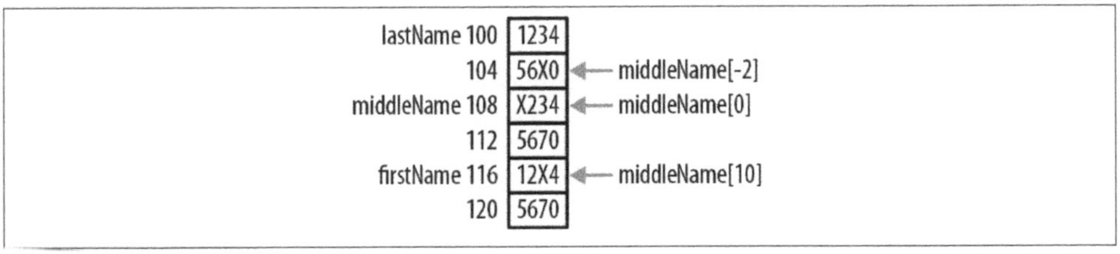

Figure 7-2. Using invalid array indexes

As explained in Chapter 4, the address calculated using subscripts does not check the index values. This is a simple case of buffer overflow.

Calculating the Array Size Incorrectly

When passing an array to a function, always pass the size of the array at the same time. This information will help the function avoid exceeding the bounds of the array. In the replace function shown below, the string's address is passed along with a replacement character and the buffer's size. The function's purpose is to replace all of the characters in the string up to the NUL character with the replacement character. The size argument prevents the function from writing past the end of the buffer:

```c
void replace(char buffer[], char replacement, size_t size) {
    size_t count = 0;
    while(*buffer != NUL && count++<size) {
        *buffer = replacement;
        buffer++;
    }
}
```

In the following sequence, the name array can only hold up to seven characters plus the NUL termination character. However, we purposely write past the end of the array to demonstrate the replace function. In the following sequence, the replace function is passed to the name and a replacement character of +:

```c
char name[8];
strcpy(name,"Alexander");
```

```
replace(name,'+',sizeof(name));
printf("%s\n", name);
```

When this code is executed, we get the following output:

```
+++++++++r
```

Only eight plus-sign characters were added to the array. While the strcpy function permitted buffer overflow, the replace function did not. This assumes that the size passed is valid. Functions like strcpy that do not pass the buffer's size should be used with caution. Passing the buffer's size provides an additional layer of protection.

Misusing the sizeof Operator

An example of misusing the sizeof operator occurs when we attempt to check our pointer bounds but do it incorrectly. In the following example, we allocate memory for an integer array and then initialize each element to 0.

```
int buffer[20];
int *pbuffer = buffer;
for(int i=0; i<sizeof(buffer); i++) {
    *(pbuffer++) = 0;
}
```

However, the sizeof(buffer) expression returns 80 since the size of the buffer in bytes is 80 (20 multiplied by 4 byte elements). The for loop is executed 80 times instead of 20 and will frequently result in a memory access exception terminating the application. Avoid this by using the expression sizeof(buffer)/sizeof(int) in the test condition of the for statement.

Always Match Pointer Types

It is a good idea to always use the appropriate pointer type for the data. To demonstrate one possible pitfall, consider the following sequence. A pointer to an integer is assigned to a pointer to a short:

```
int  num = 2147483647;
int *pi = &num;
short *ps = (short*)pi;
printf("pi: %p  Value(16): %x  Value(10): %d\n", pi, *pi, *pi);
printf("ps: %p  Value(16): %hx  Value(10): %hd\n",
        ps, (unsigned short)*ps, (unsigned short)*ps);
```

The output of the snippet follows:

```
pi: 100  Value(16): 7fffffff  Value(10): 2147483647
ps: 100  Value(16): ffff  Value(10): -1
```

Notice that it appears that the first hexadecimal digit stored at address 100 is 7 or f, depending on whether it is displayed as an integer or as a short. This apparent contradiction is an artifact of executing this sequence on a little endian machine. The layout of memory for the constant at address 100 is illustrated in Figure 7-3.

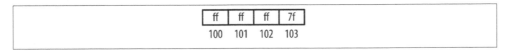

Figure 7-3. Mismatched pointer types

If we treat this as a short number and only use the first two bytes, then we get the short value of –1. If we treat this as an integer and use all four bytes, then we get 2,147,483,647. These types of subtle problems are what make C and pointers such a challenging subject.

Bounded Pointers

The term *bounded pointers* describes pointers whose use is restricted to only valid regions. For example, with an array declared with 32 elements, a pointer used with this array would be restricted from accessing any memory before or after the array.

C does not provide any direct support for this approach. However, it can be enforced explicitly by the programmer, as shown below:

```
#define SIZE 32

char name[SIZE];
char *p = name;
if(name != NULL) {
    if(p >= name && p < name+SIZE) {
        // Valid pointer - continue
    } else {
        // Invalid pointer - error condition
    }
}
```

This approach can get tedious. Instead, static analysis as discussed in the section "Using Static Analysis Tools" on page 173 can be helpful.

An interesting variation is to create a pointer validation function (*http://bit.ly/ZeU1aO*). For this to happen, the initial location and range must be known.

Another approach is to use the Bounded Model Checking (*http://www.cprover.org/cbmc/*) for ANSI-C and C++ (CBMC). This application checks for various safety and security issues within C programs and finds array bounds and buffer overflow problems.

 Smart pointers, available in C++, provide a way of simulating a pointer and support bounds checking. Unfortunately, they are not available in C.

String Security Issues

Security issues related to a string generally occur when we write past the end of a string. In this section, we will focus on the "standard" functions that contribute to this problem.

The use of string functions such as `strcpy` and `strcat` can result in buffer overflow if they are not used carefully. Several approaches have been suggested to replace these methods, but none have become widely accepted. The `strncpy` and `strncat` functions can provide some support for this operation where a `size_t` parameter specifies the maximum number of characters to copy. However, they can also be error prone if the number of characters is not calculated correctly.

In C11 (Annex K), the `strcat_s` and `strcpy_s` functions have been added. They return an error if buffer overflow occurs. Currently, they are only supported by Microsoft Visual C++. The following example illustrates the use of the `strcpy_s` function. It takes three parameters: a destination buffer, the size of the destination buffer, and a source buffer. If the return value is zero, then no errors occurred. However, in this example, an error will result since the source is too large to fit into the destination buffer:

```
char firstName [8];
int result;
result = strcpy_s(firstName,sizeof(firstName),"Alexander");
```

The `scanf_s` and `wscanf_s` functions are also available to protect against buffer overflow.

The `gets` function reads a string from standard input and stores the character in a designated buffer. It can write past the buffer's declared length. If the string is too long, then buffer overflow will occur.

Also, the `strlcpy` and `strlcat` functions are supported on some Linux systems but not by GNU C library. They are thought by some to create more problems than they solve and are not well documented.

The use of some functions can result in an attacker accessing memory using a technique known as *format string attacks*. In these attacks, a user-supplied format string, illustrated below, is crafted to enable access to memory and potentially the ability to inject code. In this simple program, the second command line argument is used as the first parameter of the `printf` function:

```
int main(int argc, char** argv) {
    printf(argv[1]);
    ...
}
```

This program can be executed using a command similar to the following:

```
main.exe "User Supplied Input"
```

Its output will appear as:

```
User Supplied Input
```

Although this program is innocuous, a more sophisticated attack can do real damage. Comprehensive coverage of this topic is not provided here; however, more detail on how to effect such an attack can be found at hackerproof.org (*http://bit.ly/YQXDj5*).

Functions such as printf, fprintf, snprintf, and syslog all have a format string as an argument. The simplest defense against this type of attack is to never use a user-supplied format string with these functions.

Pointer Arithmetic and Structures

Pointer arithmetic should only be used with arrays. Because arrays are guaranteed to be allocated in a contiguous block of memory, pointer arithmetic will result in a valid offset. However, they should not be used within structures, as the structure's fields may not be allocated in consecutive regions of memory.

This is illustrated with the following structure. The name field is allocated 10 bytes, and is followed by an integer. However, since the integer will be aligned on a four-byte boundary, there will be a gap between the two fields. Gaps of this type are explained in the section "How Memory Is Allocated for a Structure" on page 135.

```
typedef struct _employee {
    char name[10];
    int age;
} Employee;
```

The following sequence attempts to use a pointer to access the age field of the structure:

```
Employee employee;
// Initialize eployee
char *ptr = employee.name;
ptr += sizeof(employee.name);
```

The pointer will contain the address 110, which is the address of the two bytes found between the two fields. Dereferencing the pointer will interpret the four bytes at address 110 as an integer. This is illustrated in Figure 7-4.

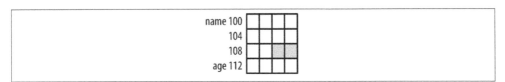

Figure 7-4. Structure padding example

Improperly aligned pointers can result in an abnormal program termination or retrieval of bad data. In addition, slower pointer access is possible if the compiler is required to generate additional machine code to compensate for the improper alignment.

Even if the memory within a structure is contiguous, it is not a good practice to use pointer arithmetic with the structure's fields. The following structure defines an Item consisting of three integers. While the three integer fields will normally be allocated in consecutive memory locations, there is no guarantee that they will be:

```
typedef struct _item {
    int partNumber;
    int quantity;
    int binNumber;
}Item;
```

The following code sequence declares a part and then uses pointer arithmetic to access each field:

```
Item part = {12345, 35, 107};
int *pi = &part.partNumber;
printf("Part number: %d\n",*pi);
pi++;
printf("Quantity: %d\n",*pi);
pi++;
printf("Bin number: %d\n",*pi);
```

Normally, the output will be as expected, but it is not guaranteed to work. A better approach is to assign each field to pi:

```
int *pi = &part.partNumber;
printf("Part number: %d\n",*pi);
pi = &part.quantity;
printf("Quantity: %d\n",*pi);
pi = &part.binNumber;
printf("Bin number: %d\n",*pi);
```

Even better, do not use pointers at all, as shown below:

```
printf("Part number: %d\n",part.partNumber);
printf("Quantity: %d\n",part.quantity);
printf("Bin number: %d\n",part.binNumber);
```

Function Pointer Issues

Functions and function pointers are used to control a program's execution sequence, but they can be misused, resulting in unpredictable behavior. Consider the use of the function getSystemStatus. This function returns an integer value that reflects the system's status:

```
int getSystemStatus() {
    int status;
    ...
    return status;
}
```

The best way to determine whether the system status is zero follows:

```
if(getSystemStatus() == 0) {
    printf("Status is 0\n");
} else {
    printf("Status is not 0\n");
}
```

In the next example, we forget to use the open and close parentheses. The code will not execute properly:

```
if(getSystemStatus == 0) {
    printf("Status is 0\n");
} else {
    printf("Status is not 0\n");
}
```

The else clause will always be executed. In the logical expression, we compared the address of the function with 0 instead of calling the function and comparing its return value to 0. Remember, when a function name is used by itself, it returns the address of the function.

A similar mistake is using a function return value directly without comparing its result to some other value. The address is simply returned and evaluated as true or false. The address of the function is not likely to be zero. As a result, the address returned will be evaluated as true since C treats any nonzero value as true:

```
if(getSystemStatus) {
    // Will always be true
}
```

We should have written the function call as follows to determine whether the status is zero.

```
if(getSystemStatus()) {
```

Do not assign a function to a function pointer when their signatures differ. This can result in undefined behavior. An example of this misuse is shown below:

```
int (*fptrCompute)(int,int);
int add(int n1, int n2, int n3) {
    return n1+n2+n3;
}

fptrCompute = add;
fptrCompute(2,5);
```

We attempted to invoke the add function with only two arguments when it expected three arguments. This will compile, but the output is indeterminate.

A function pointer executes different functions, depending on the address assigned to it. For example, we may want to use the printf function for normal operations but change it to a different function for specialized logging purposes. Declaring and using such a function pointer is shown below:

```
int (*fptrIndirect)(const char *, ...) = printf;
fptrIndirect("Executing printf indirectly");
```

It may be possible for an attacker to use buffer overflow to overwrite the function pointer's address. When this happens, control can be transferred to an arbitrary location in memory.

Memory Deallocation Issues

Even when memory has been deallocated, we are not necessarily through with the pointer or the deallocated memory. One concern deals with what happens when we try to free the same memory twice. In addition, once memory is freed, we may need to be concerned with protecting any residual data. We will examine these issues in this section.

Double Free

Freeing a block of memory twice is referred to as double free, as explained in "Double Free" on page 48. The following illustrates how this can be done:

```
char *name = (char*)malloc(...);
...
free(name);      // First free
...
free(name);      // Double free
```

In an earlier version of the zlib compression library, it was possible for a double-free operation to result in a denial of service attack or possibly to insert code into the program. However, this is extremely unlikely and the vulnerability has been addressed in newer releases of the library. More information about this vulnerability can be found at cert.org (*http://bit.ly/10vpVxM*).

A simple technique to avoid this type of vulnerability is to always assign NULL to a pointer after it has been freed. Subsequent attempts to free a null pointer will be ignored by most heap managers.

```
char *name = (char*)malloc(...);
...
free(name);
name = NULL;
```

In the section "Writing your own free function" on page 70, we developed a function to achieve this effect.

Clearing Sensitive Data

It is a good idea to overwrite sensitive data in memory once it is no longer needed. When your application terminates, most operating systems do not zero out or otherwise manipulate the memory used by your application. Your old space may be allocated to another program, which will have access to its contents. Overwriting sensitive data will make it more difficult for another program to extract useful information from program address space previously used to hold sensitive data. The following sequence illustrates zeroing out of sensitive data in a program:

```
char name[32];
int userID;
char *securityQuestion;

// assign values
...

// Delete sensitive information
memset(name,0,sizeof(name));
userID = 0;
memset(securityQuestion,0,strlen(securityQuestion));
```

If name has been declared as a pointer, then we should clear its memory before we deallocate it, as shown below:

```
char *name = (char*)malloc(...);
...
memset(name,0,sizeof(name));
free(name);
```

Using Static Analysis Tools

Numerous static analysis tools are available to detect improper use of pointers. In addition, most compilers possess options to detect many of the issues addressed in this chapter. For example, the GCC compiler's -Wall option enables the reporting of all compiler warnings.

The following illustrates the warnings produced by some of the examples included in this chapter. Here we forget to use open and close parentheses for a function call:

```
if(getSystemStatus == 0) {
```

The result is the following warning:

```
warning: the address of 'getSystemStatus' will never be NULL
```

We make essentially the same mistake here:

```
        if(getSystemStatus) {
```

However, the warning is different:

```
warning: the address of 'getSystemStatus' will always evaluate as 'true'
```

Using incompatible pointer types will result in a warning:

```
int (*fptrCompute)(int,int);
int addNumbers(int n1, int n2, int n3) {
    return n1+n2+n3;
}

    ...
    fptrCompute = addNumbers;
```

The warning follows:

```
warning: assignment from incompatible pointer type
```

Failure to initialize a pointer is usually a problem:

```
    char *securityQuestion;
    strcpy(securityQuestion,"Name of your home town");
```

The warning generated is surprisingly lucid:

```
warning: 'securityQuestion' is used uninitialized in this function
```

Numerous static analysis tools are also available. Some are free, and others are available for a fee. They generally provide enhanced diagnostic capabilities beyond those provided by most compilers. Because of their complex nature, examples are beyond the scope of this book.

Summary

In this chapter, we investigated how pointers can affect an application's security and reliability. These issues were organized around the declaration and initialization of pointers, the use of pointers, and memory deallocation problems. For example, it is important to initialize a pointer before it is used and to potentially clean up the memory used by a string once the memory is no longer needed. Setting a pointer to NULL can be an effective technique in many of these situations.

Pointers can be misused in several ways. Many of these involve overwriting memory outside the string, a form of buffer overflow. The misuse of pointers can cause undefined behavior in several areas, including mismatching pointer types and incorrect pointer arithmetic.

We illustrated various techniques to avoid these types of problems. Many involved simply understanding how pointers and strings are supposed to be used. We also touch on how compilers and static analysis tools can be used to identify potential problem areas.

CHAPTER 8

Odds and Ends

Pointers are vital to almost all aspects of C. Many of these areas are fairly well defined, such as arrays and functions. This chapter examines several topics that do not neatly fit into the previous chapters. Coverage of these topics will round out your knowledge of how pointers work.

In this chapter, we will examine several topics related to pointers:

- Casting pointers
- Accessing hardware devices
- Aliasing and strict aliasing
- Use of the `restrict` keyword
- Threads
- Object-oriented techniques

With regards to threads, there are two areas of interest. The first deals with the basic problem of sharing data between threads using pointers. The second discusses how pointers are used to support callbacks. An operation may invoke a function to perform a task. When the actual function called changes, this is referred to as a callback function. For example, the sort function used in Chapter 5 is an example of a callback function. A callback is also used to communicate between threads.

We will cover two approaches for providing object-oriented type support within C. The first is the use of an opaque pointer. This technique hides a data structure's implementation details from users. The second technique will demonstrate how to effect polymorphic type behavior in C.

Casting Pointers

Casting is a basic operator that can be quite useful when used with pointers. Casting pointers are useful for a number of reasons, including:

- Accessing a special purpose address
- Assigning an address to represent a port
- Determining a machine's endianness

We will also address a topic closely related to casting in the section "Using a Union to Represent a Value in Multiple Ways" on page 182.

 The endianness of a machine generally refers to the order of bytes within a data type. Two common types of endian include little endian and big endian. Little endian means the low-order bytes are stored in the lowest address, while big endian means the high-order bytes are stored at the lowest address.

We can cast an integer to a pointer to an integer as shown below:

```
int num = 8;
int *pi = (int*)num;
```

However, this is normally a poor practice as it allows access to an arbitrary address, potentially a location the program is not permitted to access. This is illustrated in Figure 8-1, where address 8 is not in the application's address space. If the pointer is dereferenced, it will normally result in the application's termination.

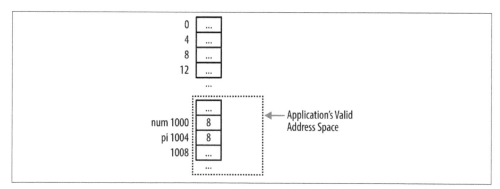

Figure 8-1. Casting an integer to a bad location

For some situations, such as when we need to address memory location zero, we may need to cast a pointer to an integer and then cast it back to a pointer. This is more common on older systems where a pointer's size is the same size as an integer. However, this does not always work. The approach is illustrated below, where the output is implementation-dependent:

```
pi = &num;
printf("Before: %p\n",pi);
int tmp = (int)pi;
pi = (int*)tmp;
printf("After: %p\n",pi);
```

Casting a pointer to an integer and then back to a pointer has never been considered good practice. If this needs to be done, consider using a union, as discussed in the section"Using a Union to Represent a Value in Multiple Ways" on page 182.

Remember that casting to and from an integer is different from casting to and from void, as illustrated in "Pointer to void" on page 14.

 The term *handle* is sometimes confused with a pointer. A handle is a reference to a system resource. Access to the resource is provided through the handle. However, the handle generally does not provide direct access to the resource. In contrast, a pointer contains the resource's address.

Accessing a Special Purpose Address

The need to access a special purpose address often occurs on embedded systems where there is minimal operating system mediation. For example, in some low-level OS kernels the address of video RAM for a PC is 0xB8000. This address holds the character to be displayed in the first row and first column when in text mode. We can assign this address to a pointer and then assign a character to the location, as illustrated below. The memory layout is shown in Figure 8-2:

```
#define VIDEO_BASE 0xB8000
int *video = (int *) VIDEO_BASE;
*video = 'A';
```

If appropriate, the address can also be read. This is not typically done for video memory.

When you need to address memory at location zero, sometimes the compiler will treat it as a NULL pointer value. Access to location zero is often needed in low-level kernel programs. Here are a few techniques to address this situation:

- Set the pointer to zero (this does not always work)
- Assign a zero to an integer and then cast the integer to the pointer

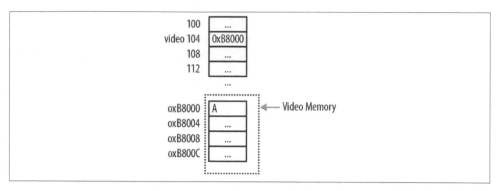

Figure 8-2. Addressing video memory on a PC

- Use a union as discussed in the section "Using a Union to Represent a Value in Multiple Ways" on page 182

- Use the memset function to assign a zero to the pointer

An example of using the memset function follows. Here, the memory referenced by ptr is set to all zeros:

```
memset((void*)&ptr, 0, sizeof(ptr));
```

On systems where addressing memory location zero is needed, the vendor will frequently have a workaround.

Accessing a Port

A port is both a hardware and a software concept. Servers use software ports to indicate they should receive certain messages sent to the machine. A hardware port is typically a physical input/output system component connected to an external device. By either reading or writing to a hardware port, information and commands can be processed by the program.

Typically, software that accesses a port is part of the OS. The following illustrates the use of pointers to access a port:

```
#define PORT 0xB0000000
unsigned int volatile * const port = (unsigned int *) PORT;
```

The machine uses the hexadecimal value address to designate a port. The data is treated as an unsigned integer. The volatile keyword qualifier indicates that the variable can be changed outside of the program. For example, an external device may write data to a port. This write operation is performed independent of the computer's processor. Compilers will sometimes temporarily use a cache, or register, to hold the value in a memory location for optimization purposes. If the external write modifies the memory location, then this change will not be reflected in the cached or register value.

Using the volatile keyword will prevent the runtime system from using a register to temporarily store the port value. Each port access requires the system to read or write to the port instead of reading a possibly stale value stored in a register. We don't want to declare all variables as volatile, as this will prevent the compiler from performing certain types of optimizations.

The application can then read or write to the port by dereferencing the port pointer as follows. The layout of memory is shown in Figure 8-3, where the External Device can read/write to the memory at 0xB0000000:

```
*port = 0x0BF4; // write to the port
value = *port; // read from the port
```

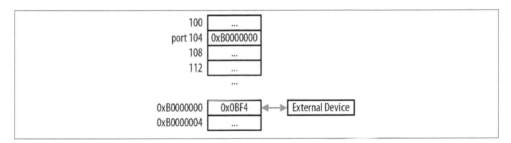

Figure 8-3. Accessing a port

 It is not a good idea to access volatile memory with a nonvolatile variable. Using such a variable can result in undefined behavior.

Accessing Memory using DMA

Direct Memory Access (DMA) is a low-level operation that assists in transferring data between main memory and some device. It is not part of the ANSI C specification but operating systems typically provide support for this operation. DMA operations are normally conducted in parallel with the CPU. This frees up the CPU for other processing and can result in better performance.

The programmer will invoke a DMA function and then wait for the operation's completion. Often, a callback function is provided by the programmer. When the operation completes, the callback function is invoked by the operating system. The callback function is specified using a function pointer and is discussed further in the section "Using Function Pointers to Support Callbacks" on page 188.

Determining the Endianness of a Machine

The cast operator can also be used to determine the endianness of architecture. *Endian* refers to the order of bytes in a unit of memory. The endianness is usually referred to as either *little endian* or *big endian*. For example, for a four-byte representation of an integer using little endian ordering, the integer's least significant byte is stored in the lowest address of the four bytes.

In the following example, we cast an integer's address as a pointer to a char. The individual bytes are then displayed:

```
int num = 0x12345678;
char* pc = (char*) &num;
for (int i = 0; i < 4; i++) {
    printf("%p: %02x \n", pc, (unsigned char) *pc++);
}
```

The output of this code snippet as executed on an Intel PC reflects a little-endian architecture, as shown below. Figure 8-4 illustrates how these values are allocated in memory:

```
100: 78
101: 56
102: 34
103: 12
```

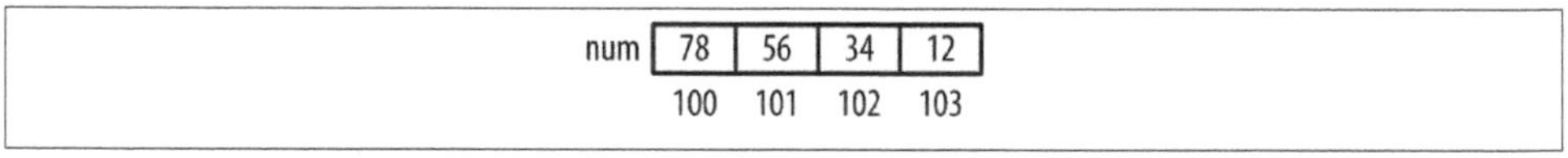

Figure 8-4. Endian example

Aliasing, Strict Aliasing, and the restrict Keyword

One pointer is said to alias another pointer if they both reference the same memory location. This is not uncommon, and it can present a number of problems. In the following code sequence, two pointers are declared and are both assigned the same address:

```
int num = 5;
int* p1 = &num;
int* p2 = &num;
```

When the compiler generates code for pointers, it has to assume that aliasing may occur unless told otherwise. The use of aliasing imposes restrictions on compiler-generated code. If two pointers reference the same location, either can potentially modify that location. When the compiler generates code to read or write to that location, it is not always able to optimize the code by storing the value in a register. It is forced to perform machine-level load and store operations with each reference. The repeated load/store sequence can be inefficient. In some situations, the compiler must also be concerned about the order in which the operations are performed.

Strict aliasing is another form of aliasing. Strict aliasing does not allow a pointer of one data type to alias a pointer of a different data type. In the following code sequence, a pointer to an integer aliases a pointer to a float. This violates the strict aliasing rule. The sequence determines whether the number is negative. Instead of comparing its argument to zero to see whether it is positive, this approach will execute faster:

```
float number = 3.25f;
unsigned int *ptrValue = (unsigned int *)&number;
unsigned int result = (*ptrValue & 0x80000000) == 0;
```

 Strict aliasing does not apply to pointers differing only by sign or qualifier. The following are all valid strict aliases:

```
int num;
const int *ptr1 = &num;
int *ptr2 = &num;
int volatile ptr3 = &num;
```

However, there are situations where the ability to use multiple representations of the same data can be useful. To avoid aliasing problems, several techniques are available:

- Use a union
- Disable strict aliasing
- Use a pointer to char

A union of two data types can get around the strict aliasing problem. This is discussed in the section "Using a Union to Represent a Value in Multiple Ways" on page 182. If your compiler has an option to disable strict aliasing, it can be turned off. The GCC compiler has the following compiler options:

- -fno-strict-aliasing to turn it off
- -fstrict-aliasing to turn it on
- -Wstrict-aliasing to warn of strict aliasing-related problems

Code requiring strict aliasing to be turned off probably reflects poor memory access practices. When possible, take time to resolve these issues instead of turning off strict aliasing.

Compilers do not always do a good job at reporting alias-related warnings. They can sometimes miss aliases and may sometimes report alias problems where they don't exist. It is ultimately up to the programmer to identify alias conditions.

A pointer to char is always assumed to potentially alias any object. Thus, it can be used safely in most situations. However, casting a pointer to one data type to a pointer to char and then casting the pointer to char to a second pointer data type will result in undefined behavior and should be avoided.

Using a Union to Represent a Value in Multiple Ways

C is a typed language. When a variable is declared, a type is assigned to it. Multiple variables can exist with different types. At times, it may be desirable to convert one type to another type. This is normally achieved with casting but can also be performed using a union. The term *type punning* describes the technique used to subvert the type system.

When the conversion involves pointers, serious problems can result. To illustrate this technique, we will use three different functions. These will determine whether a floating point number is positive.

The first function shown below uses a union of a float and an unsigned integer. The function first assigns the floating point value to the union and then extracts the integer to perform the test:

```
typedef union _conversion {
    float fNum;
    unsigned int uiNum;
} Conversion;

int isPositive1(float number) {
    Conversion conversion = { .fNum =number};
    return (conversion.uiNum & 0x80000000) == 0;
}
```

This will work correctly and does not involve aliasing because no pointers are involved. The next version uses a union that contains pointers to the two data types. The floating point number's address is assigned to the first pointer. The integer's pointer is then dereferenced to perform the test. This violates the strict aliasing rule:

```
typedef union _conversion2 {
    float *fNum;
    unsigned int *uiNum;
} Conversion2;

int isPositive2(float number) {
    Conversion2 conversion;
    conversion.fNum =&number;
```

```
        return (*conversion.uiNum & 0x80000000) == 0;
}
```

The following function does not use a union and violates the strict aliasing rule since the ptrValue pointer shares the same address as number:

```
int isPositive3(float number) {
    unsigned int *ptrValue = (unsigned int *)&number;
    return (*ptrValue & 0x80000000) == 0;
}
```

The approach used by these functions assumes:

- The IEEE-754 floating point standard is used to represent a floating point number
- The floating number is laid out in a particular manner
- Integer and floating point pointers are aligned correctly

However, these assumptions are not always valid. While approaches such as this can optimize operations, they are not always portable. When portability is important, performing a floating point comparison is a better approach.

Strict Aliasing

A compiler does not enforce strict aliasing. It will only generate warnings. The compiler assumes that two or more pointers of different types will never reference the same object. This includes pointers to structures with different names but that are otherwise identical. With strict aliasing, the compiler is able to perform certain optimizations. If the assumption is incorrect, then unexpected results may occur.

Even if two structures have the same field but different names, two pointers to these structures should never reference the same object. In the following example, it is assumed the person and employee pointers will never reference the same object:

```
typedef struct _person {
    char* firstName;
    char* lastName;
    unsigned int age;
} Person;

typedef struct _employee {
    char* firstName;
    char* lastName;
    unsigned int age;
} Employee;

Person* person;
Employee* employee;
```

However, the pointers can reference the same object if the structure definitions differ only by their name, as illustrated below:

```
typedef struct _person {
    char* firstName;
    char* lastName;
    unsigned int age;
} Person;

typedef Person Employee;

Person* person;
Employee* employee;
```

Using the restrict Keyword

C compilers assume pointers are aliased by default. Using the restrict keyword when declaring a pointer tells the compiler that the pointer is not aliased. This allows the compiler to generate more efficient code. Frequently, this is achieved by caching the pointer. Bear in mind that this is only a recommendation. The compiler may decide not to optimize the code. If aliases are used, then the code's execution will result in undefined behavior. The compiler will not provide any warning when the assumption is violated.

 New code development should use the restrict keyword with most pointer declarations. This will enable better code optimization. Modifying existing code may not be worth the effort.

The following function illustrates the definition and use of the restrict keyword. The function adds two vectors together and stores the result in the first vector:

```
void add(int size, double * restrict arr1, const double * restrict arr2) {
    for (int i = 0; i < size; i++) {
        arr1[i] += arr2[i];
    }
}
```

The restrict keyword is used with both array parameters, but they should not both reference the same block of memory. The following shows the correct usage of the function:

```
double vector1[] = {1.1, 2.2, 3.3, 4.4};
double vector2[] = {1.1, 2.2, 3.3, 4.4};

add(4,vector1,vector2);
```

In the following sequence, the function is called improperly with the same vector being passed as both parameters. The first statement uses an alias while the second statement uses the same vector twice:

```
double vector1[] = {1.1, 2.2, 3.3, 4.4};
double *vector3 = vector1;

add(4,vector1,vector3);
add(4,vector1,vector1);
```

Though it may sometimes work correctly, the results of the function invocation may not be reliable.

Several standard C functions use the `restrict` keyword, including:

- `void *memcpy(void * restrict s1, const void * restrict s2, size_t n);`
- `char *strcpy(char * restrict s1, const char * restrict s2);`
- `char *strncpy(char * restrict s1, const char * restrict s2, size_t n);`
- `int printf(const char * restrict format, ... );`
- `int sprintf(char * restrict s, const char * restrict format, ... );`
- `int snprintf(char * restrict s, size_t n, const char * restrict for mat, ... );`
- `int scanf(const char * restrict format, ...);`

The `restrict` keyword has two implications:

1. To the compiler it means it can perform certain code optimizations
2. To the programmer it means these pointers should not be aliased; otherwise, the results of the operation are *undefined*.

Threads and Pointers

When threads share data, numerous problems can occur. One common problem is the corruption of data. One thread may write to an object but the thread may be suspended momentarily, leaving that object in an inconsistent state. Subsequently, a second thread may read that object before the first thread is able to resume. The second thread is now using an invalid or corrupted object.

Since pointers are a common way of referencing data in another thread, we will examine various issues that can adversely affect a multithreaded application. As we will see in this section's examples, mutexes are frequently used to protect data.

The C11 standard implements threading, but it is not widely supported at this time. There are numerous libraries that support threads in C. We will use *Portable Operating System Interface* (POSIX) threads since they are readily available. Regardless of the library used, the techniques presented here should be applicable.

We will use pointers to support a multithreaded application and callbacks. Threads are an involved topic. We assume you are familiar with basic thread concepts and terms, and therefore, we will not go into detail about how the POSIX thread functions work. The reader is referred to O'Reilly's PThreads Programming for a more detailed discussion of this topic.

Sharing Pointers Between Threads

When two or more threads share data, the data can become corrupted. To illustrate this problem, we will implement a multi-threaded function that computes the dot product of two vectors. The multiple threads will simultaneously access two vectors and a sum field. When the threads complete, the sum field will hold the dot product value.

The dot product of two vectors is computed by summing the product of the corresponding elements of each vector. We will use two data structures in support of the operation. The first one, VectorInfo, contains information about the two vectors being manipulated. It has pointers to the two vectors, the sum field to hold the dot product, and a length field to specify the vector segment's size used by the dot product function. The length field represents that portion of the vector that a thread will process, not the entire length of a vector:

```
typedef struct {
    double *vectorA;
    double *vectorB;
    double sum;
    int length;
} VectorInfo;
```

The second data structure, Product, contains a pointer to a VectorInfo instance and the beginning index the dot Product vector will use. We will create a new instance of this structure for each thread with a different beginning index:

```
typedef struct {
    VectorInfo *info;
    int beginningIndex;
} Product;
```

While each thread will be acting on both vectors at the same time, they will be accessing different parts of the vector, so there is no conflict there. Each thread will compute a sum for its section of the vectors. However, this sum will need to be added to the sum field of the VectorInfo structure. Since multiple threads may be accessing the sum field at the same time, it is necessary to protect this data using a *mutex* as declared below. A mutex allows only one thread to access a protected variable at a time. The following declares a mutex to protect the sum variable. It is declared at a global level to allow multiple threads to access it:

```
pthread_mutex_t mutexSum;
```

The dotProduct function is shown below. When a thread is created, this function will be called. Since we are using POSIX, it is necessary to declare this function as returning void and being passed a pointer to void. This pointer passes information to the function. We will pass an instance of the Product structure.

Within the function, variables are declared to hold the beginning and ending indexes. The for loop performs the actual multiplication and keeps a cumulative total in the total variable. The last part of the function locks the mutex, adds total to sum, and then unlocks the mutex. While the mutext is locked, no other threads can access the sum variable:

```
void dotProduct(void *prod) {
    Product *product = (Product*)prod;
    VectorInfo *vectorInfo = Product->info;
    int beginningIndex = Product->beginningIndex;
    int endingIndex = beginningIndex + vectorInfo->length;
    double total = 0;

    for (int i = beginningIndex; i < endingIndex; i++) {
        total += (vectorInfo->vectorA[i] * vectorInfo->vectorB[i]);
    }

    pthread_mutex_lock(&mutexSum);
    vectorInfo->sum += total;
    pthread_mutex_unlock(&mutexSum);

    pthread_exit((void*) 0);
}
```

The code to create the threads is shown below. Two simple vectors are declared along with an instance of VectorInfo. Each vector holds 16 elements. The length field is set to 4:

```
#define NUM_THREADS  4

void threadExample() {
    VectorInfo vectorInfo;
    double vectorA[] = {1.0, 2.0, 3.0, 4.0, 5.0, 6.0, 7.0, 8.0,
        9.0, 10.0, 11.0, 12.0, 13.0, 14.0, 15.0, 16.0};
    double vectorB[] = {1.0, 2.0, 3.0, 4.0, 5.0, 6.0, 7.0, 8.0,
        9.0, 10.0, 11.0, 12.0, 13.0, 14.0, 15.0, 16.0};

    double sum;

    vectorInfo.vectorA = vectorA;
    vectorInfo.vectorB = vectorB;
    vectorInfo.length = 4;
```

A four-element array of threads is created next, along with code to initialize the mutex and an attribute field for the thread:

```
pthread_t threads[NUM_THREADS];

void *status;
pthread_attr_t attr;

pthread_mutex_init(&mutexSum, NULL);
pthread_attr_init(&attr);
pthread_attr_setdetachstate(&attr, PTHREAD_CREATE_JOINABLE);

int returnValue;
int threadNumber;
```

With each for loop iteration, a new instance of the Product structure is created. It is assigned the address of vectorInfo and a unique index based on threadNumber. The threads are then created:

```
for (threadNumber = 0; threadNumber < NUM_THREADS; threadNumber++) {
    Product *product = (Product*) malloc(sizeof(Product));
    product->beginningIndex = threadNumber * 4;
    product->info = &vectorInfo;
    returnValue = pthread_create(&threads[threadNumber], &attr,
                        dotProduct, (void*) (product));
    if (returnValue) {
        printf("ERROR; Unable to create thread: %d\n", returnValue);
        exit(-1);
    }
}
```

After the for loop, the thread attribute and mutex variables are destroyed. The for loop ensures the program will wait until all four threads have completed. The dot product is then displayed. For the above vectors, the product is 1496:

```
pthread_attr_destroy(&attr);

for (int i = 0; i < NUM_THREADS; i++) {
    pthread_join(threads[i], &status);
}

pthread_mutex_destroy(&mutexSum);
printf("Dot Product sum: %lf\n", vectorInfo.sum);
pthread_exit(NULL);

}
```

The sum field is thus protected.

Using Function Pointers to Support Callbacks

We previously used a callback function in the sort function developed in Chapter 5. Since the sort example does not use multiple threads, some programmers do not call this a callback function. A more widely accepted definition of a callback is when an event in one thread results in the invocation, or callback, of a function in another thread. One thread is passed a function pointer to a callback function. An event in the function can trigger a call to the callback function. This approach is useful in GUI applications to handle user thread events.

We will illustrate this approach using a function to compute the factorial of a number. The function will callback a second function when the factorial has been computed. Information regarding the factorial is encapsulated in a FactorialData structure and is passed between the functions. This structure and the factorial function are shown below. The data consists of the factorial number, the results, and a function pointer for the callback. The factorial function uses this data to compute the factorial, store the answer in the result field, call the callback function, and then terminate the thread:

```
typedef struct _factorialData {
    int number;
    int result;
    void (*callBack)(struct _factorialData*);
} FactorialData;

void factorial(void *args) {
    FactorialData *factorialData = (FactorialData*) args;
    void (*callBack)(FactorialData*); // Function prototype

    int number = factorialData->number;
    callBack = factorialData->callBack;

    int num = 1;
    for(int i = 1; i<=number; i++) {
        num *= i;
    }

    factorialData->result = num;
    callBack(factorialData);

    pthread_exit(NULL);
}
```

The thread is created in a startThread function as shown below. The thread executes the factorial function and passes it factorial data:

```
void startThread(FactorialData *data) {
    pthread_t thread_id;
    int thread = pthread_create(&thread_id, NULL, factorial, (void *) data);
}
```

The callback function simply displays the factorial results:

```
void callBackFunction(FactorialData *factorialData) {
    printf("Factorial is %d\n", factorialData->result);
}
```

The factorial data is initialized and the `startThread` function is called as shown below. The `Sleep` function provides time for all of the threads to terminate properly:

```
FactorialData *data =
    (FactorialData*) malloc(sizeof(FactorialData));

if(!data) {
    printf("Failed to allocate memory\n");
    return;
}

data->number = 5;
data->callBack = callBackFunction;

startThread(data);

Sleep(2000);
```

When this is executed, the output will be as follows:

```
Factorial is 120
```

Instead of sleeping, the program can perform other tasks. The program does not have to wait for the thread to complete.

Object-Oriented Techniques

C is not known for its support of object-oriented programming. However, you can use C to encapsulate data using an opaque pointer and to support a certain level of polymorphic behavior. By hiding a data structure's implementation and its supporting functions, the user does not need to know how the structure is implemented. Hiding this information will reduce what the user needs to know and thus reduce the application's complexity level. In addition, the user will not be tempted to take advantage of the structure's internal details, potentially causing later problems if the data structure's implementation changes.

Polymorphic behavior helps make an application more maintainable. A polymorphic function behavior depends on the object it is executing against. This means we can add functionality to an application more easily.

Creating and Using an Opaque Pointer

An opaque pointer can be used to effect data encapsulation in C. One approach declares a structure without any implementation details in a header file. Functions are then defined to work with a specific implementation of the data structure in an implementation file. A user of the data structure will see the declaration and the functions' prototypes. However, the implementation is hidden (in the *.c/.obj* file).

Only the information needed to use the data structure is made visible to the user. If too much internal information is made available, the user may incorporate this information and become dependent on it. Should the internal structure change, then it may break the user's code.

We will develop a linked list to demonstrate an opaque pointer. The user will use one function to obtain a pointer to a linked list. This pointer can then be used to add and remove information from the linked list. The details of the linked list's internal structure and its supporting function are not available to the user. The only aspects of this structure are provided through a header file, as shown below:

```
//link.h

typedef void *Data;
typedef struct _linkedList LinkedList;

LinkedList* getLinkedListInstance();
void removeLinkedListInstance(LinkedList* list);
void addNode(LinkedList*, Data);
Data removeNode(LinkedList*);
```

Data is declared as a pointer to void. This allows the implementation to handle any type of data. The type definition for LinkedList identifies a structure called _linkedList. The definition of this structure is hidden from the user in its implementation file.

Four methods are provided to permit the use of the linked list. The user will begin by obtaining a LinkedList's instance using the getLinkedListInstance function. Once the linked list is no longer needed, the removeLinkedListInstance function should be called. Passing linked list pointers allows the functions to work with one or more linked lists.

To add data to the linked list, the addNode function is used. It is passed the linked list to use and a pointer to the data to add to the linked list. The removeNode method returns the data found at the head of the linked list.

The linked list's implementation is found in a separate file called *link.c*. The first part of the implementation, as shown below, declares variables to hold the user's data and to connect to the next node in the linked list. This is followed by the _linkedList structure's definition. In this simple linked list, only a head pointer is used:

```
// link.c

#include <stdlib.h>
#include "link.h"

typedef struct _node {
    Data* data;
    struct _node* next;
} Node;
```

```
struct _linkedList {
    Node* head;
};
```

The second part of the implementation file contains implementations of the linked list's four supporting functions. The first function returns an instance of the linked list:

```
LinkedList* getLinkedListInstance() {
    LinkedList* list = (LinkedList*)malloc(sizeof(LinkedList));
    list->head = NULL;
    return list;
}
```

The removeLinkedListInstance function's implementation follows. It will free each node in the linked list, if any, and then free the list itself. This implementation can result in a memory leak if the data referenced by the node contains pointers. One solution is to pass a function to deallocate the members of the data:

```
void removeLinkedListInstance(LinkedList* list) {
    Node *tmp = list->head;
    while(tmp != NULL) {
        free(tmp->data);   // Potential memory leak!
        Node *current = tmp;
        tmp = tmp->next;
        free(current);
    }
    free(list);
}
```

The addNode function adds the data passed as the second parameter to the linked list specified by the first parameter. Memory is allocated for the node, and the user's data is associated with the node. In this implementation, the linked list's nodes are always added to its head:

```
void addNode(LinkedList* list, Data data) {
    Node *node = (Node*)malloc(sizeof(Node));
    node->data = data;
    if(list->head == NULL) {
        list->head = node;
        node->next = NULL;
    } else {
        node->next = list->head;
        list->head = node;
    }
}
```

The removeNode function returns the data associated with the first node in the linked list. The head pointer is adjusted to point to the next node in the linked list. The data is returned and the old head node is freed, releasing it back to the heap.

This approach eliminates the need for the user to remember to free nodes of the linked list, thus avoiding a memory leak. This is a significant advantage of hiding implementation details:

```
Data removeNode(LinkedList* list) {
    if(list->head == NULL) {
        return NULL;
    } else {
        Node* tmp = list->head;
        Data* data;
        list->head = list->head->next;
        data = tmp->data;
        free(tmp);
        return data;
    }
}
```

To demonstrate the use of this data structure, we will reuse the Person structure and its functions developed in "Introduction" on page 133. The following sequence will add two people to a linked list and then remove them. First, the getLinkedListInstance function is invoked to obtain a linked list. Next, instances of Person are created using the initializePerson function and then added to the linked list using the addNode function. The displayPerson function displays the persons returned by the remove Node functions. The linked list is then freed:

```
#include "link.h";
...
    LinkedList* list = getLinkedListInstance();

    Person *person = (Person*) malloc(sizeof(Person));
    initializePerson(person, "Peter", "Underwood", "Manager", 36);
    addNode(list, person);
    person = (Person*) malloc(sizeof(Person));
    initializePerson(person, "Sue", "Stevenson", "Developer", 28);
    addNode(list, person);

    person = removeNode(list);
    displayPerson(*person);

    person = removeNode(list);
    displayPerson(*person);

    removeLinkedListInstance(list);
```

There are a couple of interesting aspects of this approach. We had to create an instance of the _linkedList structure in the *list.c* file. It needs to be created there because the sizeof operator cannot be used without a complete structure declaration. For example, if we had tried to allocate memory for this structure in the main function, as follows, we would get a syntax error:

```
LinkedList* list = (LinkedList*)malloc(sizeof(LinkedList));
```

The syntax error generated will be similar to the following:

```
error: invalid application of 'sizeof' to incomplete type 'LinkedList'
```

The type is incomplete because the compiler has no insight into the actual definition as found in the *list.c* file. All it sees is the _linkedList structure's type definition. It does not see the structure's implementation details.

The user's inability to see and potentially use the linked list's internal structure is restricted. Any changes to the structure are hidden from the user.

Only the signatures of the four supporting functions are visible to the user. Otherwise, the user is unable to use knowledge of their implementation or to modify them. The linked list structure and its supporting functions are encapsulated, reducing the burden on the user.

Polymorphism in C

Polymorphism in an object-oriented language such as C++ is based on inheritance between a base and a derived class. Since C does not support inheritance we need to simulate inheritance between structures. We will define and use two structures to illustrate polymorphic behavior. A Shape structure will represent a base "class" and a Rectangle structure will be derived from the base Shape.

The structure's variable allocation order has a large impact on how this technique works. When an instance of a derived class/structure is created, the base class/structure's variables are allocated first, followed by the derived class/structure's variables. As we will see, we also need to account for the functions we plan to override.

 Understanding how memory is allocated for objects instantiated from a class is key to understanding how inheritance and polymorphism work in an object-oriented language. The same is true when we use this technique in C.

Let's start with the Shape structure's definition as shown below. First, we allocate a structure to hold the function pointers for the structure. Next, integers are declared for an x and a y position:

```
typedef struct _shape {
    vFunctions functions;
    // Base variables
    int x;
```

```
    int y;
} Shape;
```

The vFunction structure and its supporting declarations are defined below. When a function is executed against a class/structure, its behavior will depend on what it is executing against. For example, when a display function is executed against a Shape, then a Shape should be displayed. When it is executed against a Rectangle, then a Rectangle should be displayed. In an object-oriented programming language this is typically achieved using a Virtual Table or VTable. The vFunction structure is intended to serve in this capacity:

```
typedef void (*fptrSet)(void*,int);
typedef int (*fptrGet)(void*);
typedef void (*fptrDisplay)();

typedef struct _functions {
    // Functions
    fptrSet setX;
    fptrGet getX;
    fptrSet setY;
    fptrGet getY;
    fptrDisplay display;
} vFunctions;
```

This structure consists of a series of function pointers. The fptrSet and fptrGet function pointers define the typical getter and setter functions for integer type data. In this case, they are used for getting and setting the x and y values for a Shape or Rectangle. The fptrDisplay function pointer defines a function that is passed void and returns void. We will use the display function to illustrate polymorphic behavior.

The Shape structure has four functions designed to work with it, as shown below. Their implementations are straightforward. To keep this example simple, in the display function, we simply print out the string "Shape." We pass the Shape instance to these functions as the first argument. This allows these functions to work with more than one instance of a Shape:

```
void shapeDisplay(Shape *shape) { printf("Shape\n");}
void shapeSetX(Shape *shape, int x) {shape->x = x;}
void shapeSetY(Shape *shape, int y) {shape->y = y;}
int shapeGetX(Shape *shape) { return shape->x;}
int shapeGetY(Shape *shape) { return shape->y;}
```

To assist in the creation of a Shape instance, we have provided a getShapeInstance function. It allocates memory for the object and the object's functions are assigned:

```
Shape* getShapeInstance() {
    Shape *shape = (Shape*)malloc(sizeof(Shape));
    shape->functions.display = shapeDisplay;
    shape->functions.setX = shapeSetX;
    shape->functions.getX = shapeGetX;
```

```
    shape->functions.setY = shapeSetY;
    shape->functions.getY = shapeGetY;
    shape->x = 100;
    shape->y = 100;
    return shape;
}
```

The following sequence demonstrates these functions:

```
Shape *sptr = getShapeInstance();
sptr->functions.setX(sptr,35);
sptr->functions.display();
printf("%d\n", sptr->functions.getX(sptr));
```

The output of this sequence is:

```
Shape
35
```

This may seem to be a lot of effort just to work with a Shape structure. We can see the real power of this approach once we create a structure derived from Shape: Rectangle. This structure is shown below:

```
typedef struct _rectangle {
    Shape base;
    int width;
    int height;
} Rectangle;
```

The memory allocated for the Rectangle structure's first field is the same as the memory allocated for a Shape structure. This is illustrated in Figure 8-5. In addition, we have added two new fields, width and height, to represent a rectangle's characteristics.

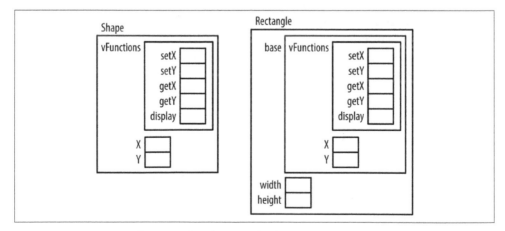

Figure 8-5. Memory allocation for shape and rectangle

Rectangle, like Shape, needs some functions associated with it. These are declared below. They are similar to those associated with the Shape structure, except that they use the Rectangle's base field:

```
void rectangleSetX(Rectangle *rectangle, int x) {
    rectangle->base.x = x;
}

void rectangleSetY(Rectangle *rectangle, int y) {
    rectangle->base.y;
}

int rectangleGetX(Rectangle *rectangle) {
    return rectangle->base.x;
}

int rectangleGetY(Rectangle *rectangle) {
    return rectangle->base.y;
}

void rectangleDisplay() {
    printf("Rectangle\n");
}
```

The getRectangleInstance function returns an instance of a Rectangle structure as follows:

```
Rectangle* getRectangleInstance() {
    Rectangle *rectangle = (Rectangle*)malloc(sizeof(Rectangle));
    rectangle->base.functions.display = rectangleDisplay;
    rectangle->base.functions.setX = rectangleSetX;
    rectangle->base.functions.getX = rectangleGetX;
    rectangle->base.functions.setY = rectangleSetY;
    rectangle->base.functions.getY = rectangleGetY;
    rectangle->base.x = 200;
    rectangle->base.y = 200;
    rectangle->height = 300;
    rectangle->width = 500;
    return rectangle;
}
```

The following illustrates the use of this structure:

```
Rectangle *rptr = getRectangleInstance();
rptr->base.functions.setX(rptr,35);
rptr->base.functions.display();
printf("%d\n", rptr->base.functions.getX(rptr));
```

The output of this sequence is:

```
Rectangle
35
```

Now let's create an array of Shape pointers and initialize them as follows. When we assign a Rectangle to shapes[1], we do not have to cast it as a (Shape*). However, we will get a warning if we don't:

```
Shape *shapes[3];
shapes[0] = getShapeInstance();
shapes[0]->functions.setX(shapes[0],35);
shapes[1] = getRectangleInstance();
shapes[1]->functions.setX(shapes[1],45);
shapes[2] = getShapeInstance();
shapes[2]->functions.setX(shapes[2],55);

for(int i=0; i<3; i++) {
    shapes[i]->functions.display();
    printf("%d\n", shapes[i]->functions.getX(shapes[i]));
}
```

When this sequence is executed, we get the following output:

```
Shape
35
Rectangle
45
Shape
55
```

While we created an array of Shape pointers, we created a Rectangle and assigned it to the array's second element. When we displayed the element in the for loop, it used the Rectangle's function behavior and not the Shape's. This is an example of polymorphic behavior. The display function depends on the structure it is executing against.

Since we are accessing it as a Shape, we should not try to access its width or height using shapes[i] since the element may or may not reference a Rectangle. If we did, then we could be accessing memory in other shapes that do not represent width or height information, yielding unpredictable results.

We can now add a second structure derived from Shape, such as a Circle, and then add it to the array without extensive modification of the code. We also need to create functions for the structure.

If we added another function to the base structure Shape, such as getArea, we could implement a unique getArea function for each class. Within a loop, we could easily add up the sum of all of the Shape and Shape-derived structures without having to first determine what type of Shape we are working with. If the Shape's implementation of getArea is sufficient, then we do not need to add one for the other structures. This makes it easy to maintain and expand an application.

Summary

In this chapter, we have explored several aspects of pointers. We started with a discussion of casting pointers. Examples illustrated how to use pointers to access memory and hardware ports. We also saw how pointers are used to determine the endianness of a machine.

Aliasing and the `restrict` keyword were introduced. Aliasing occurs when two pointers reference the same object. Compilers will assume that pointers may be aliased. However, this can result in inefficient code generation. The `restrict` keyword allows the compiler to perform better optimization.

We saw how pointers can be used with threads and learned about the need to protect data shared through pointers. In addition, we examined techniques to effect callbacks between threads using function pointers.

In the last section, we examined opaque pointers and polymorphic behavior. Opaque pointers enable C to hide data from a user. Polymorphism can be incorporated into a program to make it more maintainable.

Index

Symbols

& (ampersand), address of operator, 8, 84
* (asterisk)
    indirection (dereference) operator, 11, 20,
        35, 163–164
    in pointer declaration, 5, 20, 163–164
{} (braces), in array initialization, 81, 81, 82
[] (brackets), in array declarations, 80, 81, 82
" " (double quotes), enclosing string literals, 108
= (equal sign)
    assignment operator, 43
    initialization operator, 43
== (equal sign, double), equality operator, 20
!= (exclamation point, equal sign), inequality
    operator, 20
< (left angle bracket), less than operator, 20
<= (left angle bracket, equal sign), less than or
    equal operator, 20
- (minus sign), subtraction operator, 20
-> (minus sign, right angle bracket), points-to
    operator, 20, 134
() (parentheses)
    enclosing data type to cast, 20
    in pointer to function declarations, 11, 72
+ (plus sign), addition operator, 20
> (right angle bracket), greater than operator, 20
>= (right angle bracket, equal sign), greater than
    or equal operator, 20

' ' (single quotes), enclosing character literals,
    108
0 (zero)
    assigned to pointers, 12, 13
    as overloaded, 13

A

activation records or frames (see stack frames)
addition operator (+), 20
address of operator (&), 8, 84
Address Space Layout Randomization (ASLR),
    160
aliasing, 52, 117, 180–185
alloca function, 46
ampersand (&), address of operator, 8, 84
arithmetic operators, 20, 20–24
arrays, 79–83
    accessing memory outside of, 164–165
    array notation for, 83–85, 86, 90–92, 96, 96
    of characters, strings declared as, 109
    compared to pointers, 79, 80
    compared to pointers to arrays, 85
    declaration of, 80–83
    of function pointers, 76–76
    initialization of, 81, 81, 82
    jagged, 102–105
    multidimensional, 82
        passing to functions, 96–99
        pointers to, 94–96

We'd like to hear your suggestions for improving our indexes. Send email to index@oreilly.com.

gets function, 168
global memory, 2
global pointers, 15, 42
global variables, 33, 42
GNU compiler
    dlmalloc, 54
    RAII support, 55–56
greater than operator (>), 20
greater than or equal operator (>=), 20

H

handles, compared to pointers, 177
heap, 58–59
    corruption of
        double free causing, 49
        writing outside of memory block causing, 36
    detecting problems with, 54
    dynamic memory allocated from (see dynamic memory)
heap managers, 54–56
hidden memory leaks, 38
Hoard malloc, 54
huge pointers, 20
hyphen (-) (see minus sign (-))

I

indirection (dereference) operator (*), ix, 11, 20, 35, 163–164
    (see also dereferencing)
inequality operator (!=), 20
inheritance, 194–198
initialization of pointers, 8–9
    failure to, 161–162, 174
    to NULL, 162
initialization operator (=), 43
integers, casting to a pointer to an integer, 9
intptr_t type, 19–20

J

jagged arrays, 102–105

L

left angle bracket (<), less than operator, 20
left angle bracket, equal sign (<=), less than or equal operator, 20
less than operator (<), 20

less than or equal operator (<=), 20
linked lists, 142–149
    implementing as arrays, 3
    implementing as pointers, 3
local variables
    returning pointers to, 66–67
    stack used by, 33, 58, 59, 60
lvalue, required to be modifiable, 11, 85

M

macro definitions, declaring pointers using, 161
malloc function, 4, 34–36, 39–42
    checking return value of, 163
    creating arrays using, 86, 99–102
    implementations of, 54
    initializing strings using, 111
    overhead incurred by, 139–141
    for returning a pointer from a function, 64–66
malloca function, 46
memory
    automatic memory, 2
    dynamic memory (see dynamic memory)
    global memory, 2
    heap (see heap)
    lifetime of, 2
    scope of, 2
    special purpose addresses, accessing, 177–178
    stack (see stack)
    static memory, 2
    types of, 2
    virtual memory addresses, 10
memory leaks, 37–39
    detecting, 54
    failure to deallocate returned pointers causing, 66
    hidden, 38
    lost address causing, 37
    structure pointers not deallocated causing, 138
memory models, for C data types, 16
memset function, 43, 178
Microsoft compiler
    exception handling, 56
    malloca function, 46
    memory management, 54
minus sign (-), subtraction operator, 20

for this book, xiv
wide strings, 108
wild pointers, 161–162
wscanf_s function, 168

X

%x field specifier, printf function, 9

Z

zero (0)
  assigned to pointers, 12, 13
  as overloaded, 13

About the Author

Richard Reese has worked in the industry and in academics for the past 29 years. For 10 years, he provided software development support at Lockheed and at one point developed a C-based network application. He was a contract instructor, providing software training to industry for five years. Richard is currently an Associate Professor at Tarleton State University in Stephenville, Texas.

Colophon

The animal on the cover of *Understanding and Using C Pointers* is the piping crow-shrike, or Australian magpie (*Cracticus tibicen*). Not to be confused with the piping crow found in Indonesia, the Australian magpie is not a crow at all; it is related to butcherbirds and is native to Australia and southern New Guinea. There were once three separate species of Australian magpie, but interbreeding has resulted in the coalescence of their three species into one.

Australian magpies have black heads and bodies with varied black and white plumage on their backs, wings, and tails. The Australian magpie is also called the piping crow-shrike due to its multi-tonal, complex vocalizations. Like true crows, the Australian magpie is omnivorous, though it prefers to eat insect larvae and other invertebrates. It lives in groups of up to two dozen, and all members generally defend the group territory. During springtime, however, some breeding males will become defensive of their nests and will engage in swooping attacks on passersby, including human and their pets.

This magpie is a non-migratory bird and has adapted to human environments, as well as to a mix of forested and open areas. For that reason, it is not endangered, and although it is considered a pest species in neighboring New Zealand, the magpie may be very useful in Australia for keeping the invasive cane toad in check. When introduced to Australia, the cane toad had no natural predators, and its toxic secretions ensured the multiplication of its numbers. However, the highly intelligent magpie has learned to flip over the cane toad, pierce its underbelly, and use its long beak to eat the toad's organs, thus bypassing the poisonous skin. Researchers are hopeful that the Australian magpie will become a natural predator of the cane toad and aid in population control.

The cover image is from Wood's *Animate Creation*. The cover font is Adobe ITC Garamond. The text font is Adobe Minion Pro; the heading font is Adobe Myriad Condensed; and the code font is Dalton Maag's Ubuntu Mono.

Have it your way.

O'Reilly eBooks

- Lifetime access to the book when you buy through oreilly.com

- Provided in up to four DRM-free file formats, for use on the devices of your choice: PDF, .epub, Kindle-compatible .mobi, and Android .apk

- Fully searchable, with copy-and-paste and print functionality

- Alerts when files are updated with corrections and additions

oreilly.com/ebooks/

Safari Books Online

- Access the contents and quickly search over 7000 books on technology, business, and certification guides

- Learn from expert video tutorials, and explore thousands of hours of video on technology and design topics

- Download whole books or chapters in PDF format, at no extra cost, to print or read on the go

- Get early access to books as they're being written

- Interact directly with authors of upcoming books

- Save up to 35% on O'Reilly print books

See the complete Safari Library at safari.oreilly.com

O'REILLY®

Spreading the knowledge of innovators.

oreilly.com

©2011 O'Reilly Media, Inc. O'Reilly logo is a registered trademark of O'Reilly Media, Inc. 00000

Get even more for your money.

Join the O'Reilly Community, and register the O'Reilly books you own. It's free, and you'll get:

- $4.99 ebook upgrade offer
- 40% upgrade offer on O'Reilly print books
- Membership discounts on books and events
- Free lifetime updates to ebooks and videos
- Multiple ebook formats, DRM FREE
- Participation in the O'Reilly community
- Newsletters
- Account management
- 100% Satisfaction Guarantee

Signing up is easy:

1. **Go to: oreilly.com/go/register**
2. **Create an O'Reilly login.**
3. **Provide your address.**
4. **Register your books.**

Note: English-language books only

To order books online:
oreilly.com/store

For questions about products or an order:
orders@oreilly.com

To sign up to get topic-specific email announcements and/or news about upcoming books, conferences, special offers, and new technologies:
elists@oreilly.com

For technical questions about book content:
booktech@oreilly.com

To submit new book proposals to our editors:
proposals@oreilly.com

O'Reilly books are available in multiple DRM-free ebook formats. For more information:
oreilly.com/ebooks

Spreading the knowledge of innovators   oreilly.com

©2010 O'Reilly Media, Inc. O'Reilly logo is a registered trademark of O'Reilly Media, Inc. 00000